The Supporters' Guide

to

Welsh Football Grounds 2004

EDITOR
John Robinson

Eighth Edition

CONTENTS

Foreword 3

The Millennium Stadium, Cardiff 4

Welsh Clubs playing in the English Football League 5-7

Welsh Clubs playing in other English Leagues 8-10

Welsh Premier League Clubs 11-28

Cymru Alliance Clubs 29-46

Welsh Premier League Results and Tables for the 2002/2003 Season 47

Other Final League Tables for the 2002/2003 Season 48

Welsh Football League Division One Clubs 49-67

Welsh Football Magazine 68

Welsh Football League Division Two Clubs 69-87

Other Supporters' Guides Available 88

Welsh Football League Division Three Clubs 89-107

Wales International Statistics 2002/2003 108-110

British Library Cataloguing in Publication Data
A catalogue record for this book is available from the British Library

ISBN 1-86223-079-X

Copyright © 2003, SOCCER BOOKS LIMITED (01472 696226)
72 St. Peter's Avenue, Cleethorpes, N.E. Lincolnshire, DN35 8HU, England
Web site   http://www.soccer-books.co.uk
e-mail   info@soccer-books.co.uk

Printed by Antony Rowe Ltd.

FOREWORD

Following the Football Association of Wales' decision to discontinue the combined Official Yearbook & Supporters' Guide, we have reverted back to publishing a simple Supporters' Guide again this year. However, with the emphasis upon the clubs themselves and their history and grounds we have, for the first time, included the 2nd and 3rd Divisions of the Welsh Football League – a further 36 clubs!

Our thanks go to Bob Budd (cover artwork), Michael Robinson (page layouts), Dave Collins (Welsh Football Magazine), Gareth Davies (Wales International statistics), Ken Tucker (Welsh Football League), Alan Foulkes (Cymru Alliance) and, of course, to the many club officials for their assistance in the compilation of this guide.

Finally, we would like to wish our readers a happy and safe spectating season and on page 88 list the various other Supporters' Guides which we publish.

John Robinson
EDITOR

THE MILLENNIUM STADIUM

Re-Opened: 1999
(Formerly known as Cardiff Arms Park)
Address: Millennium Stadium, Westgate Street,
Cardiff   CF10 1JA
Ticket Office: (029) 2023-1458

Stadium Tours: (0990) 582582
Stadium Tours Shop: (029) 2082-2041
Stadium Manager: (029) 2023-1408
Pitch Size: 110 × 72 yards
Seating Capacity: 72,500

GENERAL INFORMATION
Car Parking: City Centre Car Parks
Coach Parking: Sophia Gardens
Nearest Railway Station: Cardiff Central (5-10 minutes walk)
Nearest Bus Station: Next to Railway Station
Nearest Police Station: Cardiff Centre
Police Telephone Nº: (029) 2022-2111

DISABLED INFORMATION
Disabled Sections: L4 – L14 and along the End touchlines
Disabled Toilets: Situated by the Disabled Areas
The Blind: Headsets with commentaries available
Bookings: Please phone in advance

ADMISSION INFO (2003/2004 PRICES)
Prices vary game by game

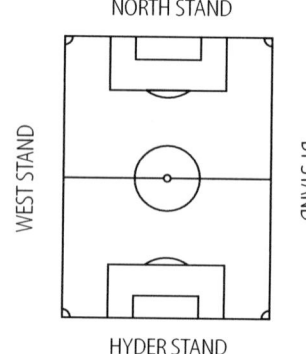

Travelling Supporters' Information:
Routes: By Car: Exit the M4 at Junction 29 and take the A48(M) following signs for Cardiff City Centre (via A470). Use the City Centre Public Car Parks; From Cardiff Central Railway Station: Proceed past the Bus Station, cross Wood Street and turn down Westgate Street (alongside the back of the Royal Hotel).

CARDIFF CITY FC

Founded: 1899 **(Entered League**: 1920)
Former Names: Riverside FC (1899-1910)
Nickname: 'Bluebirds'
Ground: Ninian Park, Sloper Road, Cardiff CF11 8SX
Record Attendance: 61,566 (14/10/61)
Ground Capacity: 21,500 (approximately)
Seating Capacity: 13,000
Pitch Size: 110 × 75 yards

Colours: Royal Blue shirts with Royal Blue shorts
Telephone Nº: (029) 2022-1001
Home Support Ticket Office: (0845) 345-1400
Away Support Ticket Office: (0845) 345-1405
Fax Number: (029) 2034-1148
Web Site: www.cardiffcityfc.co.uk

GENERAL INFORMATION

Car Parking: Leckwith Stadium car park and Street Parking
Coach Parking: Leckwith Stadium car park (adjacent)
Nearest Railway Station: Cardiff Central (1 mile)
Nearest Bus Station: Cardiff Central
Club Shop: At the ground
Opening Times: Weekdays from 9.00am to 5.00pm and Matchdays 10.00am to 3.00pm
Telephone Nº: (0845) 345-1485
Postal Sales: Yes (Internet Sales also accepted)
Police Telephone Nº: (029) 2022-2111

GROUND INFORMATION

Away Supporters' Entrances & Sections:
Grange End Visitors section entrances and accommodation (both standing and seating). Use turnstiles at Entrance F

ADMISSION INFO (2003/2004 PRICES)

Adult Standing: £13.00 – £16.00
Adult Seating: £14.00 – £20.00
Child Standing: £8.00 – £10.00
Child Seating: £6.00 – £16.00
Programme Price: £2.50

DISABLED INFORMATION

Wheelchairs: 25 spaces available for Home fans, 3 spaces for Away fans in the disabled section, Canton End Family Enclosure
Helpers: One helper admitted per disabled fan
Prices: Disabled children – free; Disabled adults – £8.00; Disabled OAPs – £8.00; Helpers – £8.00
Disabled Toilets: Yes
Contact: (0845) 345-1405 (Away fans must book in advance)

Travelling Supporters' Information:
Routes: From All Parts: Exit M4 at Junction 33 and follow Penarth (A4232) signs. After 6 miles, take the B4267 to Ninian Park.

SWANSEA CITY FC

Founded: 1900 (**Entered League**: 1920)
Former Name: Swansea Town FC (1900-1970)
Nickname: 'Swans'
Ground: Vetch Field, Swansea   SA1 3SU
Ground Capacity: 12,987
Seating Capacity: 3,416
Record Attendance: 32,796 (17/2/68)

Pitch Size: 110 × 74 yards
Colours: White shirts and shorts with Black trim
Telephone Nº: (01792) 633400
Ticket Office: (01792) 633425
Fax Number: (01792) 646120
Web Site: www.swanseacity.net

GENERAL INFORMATION

Car Parking: Kingsway (200 yards) and Clarence Terrace (50 yards) Car Parks + street parking
Coach Parking: By Police direction
Nearest Railway Station: Swansea High Street (1 mile)
Nearest Bus Station: Quadrant Depot (¼ mile)
Club Shop: 33 William Street, Swansea   SA1 3QS
Opening Times: Weekdays 10.00am – 4.30pm and Matchdays 9.30am – 5.00pm
Telephone Nº: (01792) 633425
Police Telephone Nº: (01792) 456999

GROUND INFORMATION

Away Supporters' Entrances & Sections:
Richardson Street turnstiles for the West Terrace Enclosure (partially covered)

ADMISSION INFO (2003/2004 PRICES)

Adult Standing: £11.00
Adult Seating: £13.00 – £15.00
Child/Senior Citizen Standing: £6.00 – £15.00
Child/Senior Citizen Seating: £8.00 – £15.00
Programme Price: £2.00

DISABLED INFORMATION

Wheelchairs: 9 spaces in total for Home and Away fans in the disabled section, Centre Stand touchline
Helpers: One helper admitted per wheelchair
Prices: £5.00 for the disabled
Disabled Toilets: One available
Contact: (01792) 633400   (Bookings are necessary)

Travelling Supporters' Information:
Routes: From All Parts: Exit the M4 at Junction 42 and follow Swansea (A483) signs. After 4 miles follow signs for City Centre West. After ½ mile turn right (opposite the County Hall) into West Way. At the first set of traffic lights, turn left into Glamorgan Street for Vetch Field.

WREXHAM AFC

Founded: 1872 (**Entered League**: 1921)
Nickname: 'Red Dragons'
Ground: Racecourse Ground, Mold Road, Wrexham,
North Wales   LL11 2AH
Ground Capacity: 15,500
Seating Capacity: 11,500
Record Attendance: 34,445 (26/1/57)

Pitch Size: 111 × 71 yards
Colours: Red shirts with White shorts
Telephone Nº: (01978) 262129
Ticket Office: (01978) 262129
Fax Number: (01978) 357821
Web Site: www.wrexhamafc.co.uk

GENERAL INFORMATION

Car Parking: Town car parks are nearby and also Newi
College (Mold End)
Coach Parking: By Police direction
Nearest Railway Station: Wrexham General (adjacent)
Nearest Bus Station: Wrexham (King Street)
Club Shop: At the ground, under the Sainsbury Stand
Opening Times: Office hours only
Telephone Nº: (01978) 352536
Police Telephone Nº: (01978) 290222

GROUND INFORMATION

Away Supporters' Entrances & Sections:
Turnstiles 36-42 for the Eric Roberts (Builders) Stand

ADMISSION INFO (2003/2004 PRICES)

Adult Standing: £12.00
Adult Seating: £13.00 – £15.00
Child Standing: £6.00
Child Seating: £8.00 – £10.00
Programme Price: £2.00

DISABLED INFORMATION

Wheelchairs: 35 spaces in the Pryce Griffiths Stand
Helpers: One helper admitted per wheelchair
Prices: Free for the disabled. Helpers pay £11.00
Disabled Toilets: Available in the disabled section
Contact: (01978) 351332 (Tony Millington) (Please book)

Travelling Supporters' Information:
Routes: From the North and West: Take the A483 and the Wrexham bypass to the junction with the A541. Branch left at the
roundabout and follow Wrexham signs into Mold Road; From the East: Take the A525 or A534 into Wrexham then follow the
A541 signs into Mold Road; From the South: Take the the M6, then the M54 and follow the A5 and A483 to the Wrexham bypass
and the junction with the A541. Branch right at the roundabout and follow signs for the Town Centre.

COLWYN BAY FC

Founded: 1885
Former Names: None
Nickname: 'Bay' 'Seagulls'
Ground: Llanelian Road, Old Colwyn, North Wales, LL29 8UN
Correspondence: 15 Smith Avenue, Old Colwyn, Clwyd LL29 8BE
Record Attendance: 2,500

Colours: Sky Blue shirts and shorts
Telephone Nº: (01492) 534724
Daytime Phone Nº: (01492) 542225
Fax Number: (01492) 514581
Pitch Size: 110 × 75 yards
Ground Capacity: 2,500
Seating Capacity: 500
Web site: www.cbfc.skynow.co.uk

GENERAL INFORMATION

Supporters Club: M. Mottram, 340 Abergele Road, Old Colwyn, Colwyn Bay
Telephone Nº: (01492) 515951
Car Parking: At the ground
Coach Parking: At the ground
Nearest Railway Station: Colwyn Bay (1 mile)
Nearest Bus Station: Colwyn Bay
Club Shop: At the ground
Opening Times: Matchdays only
Telephone Nº: (01492) 515951
Police Telephone Nº: (01492) 517171

GROUND INFORMATION

Away Supporters' Entrances & Sections:
No usual segregation

ADMISSION INFO (2003/2004 PRICES)

Adult Standing: £6.00
Adult Seating: £6.00
Child Standing: £3.00
Child Seating: £3.00
Programme Price: £1.00

DISABLED INFORMATION

Wheelchairs: Accommodated in Covered Terrace
Helpers: Admitted
Prices: Please phone the club for information
Disabled Toilets: Available in the Social Club
Contact: (01492) 514581 (Bookings are not necessary)

Travelling Supporters' Information:
Routes: From Queensferry: Take the A55 and when the expressway is reached take the first exit (signposted Old Colwyn). Turn left at the bottom of the slip road then straight on at the mini-roundabout into Llanelian Road. The ground is ½ mile on the right.

MERTHYR TYDFIL FC

Founded: 1945
Former Names: Merthyr Town FC
Nickname: 'Martyrs'
Ground: Penydarren Park, Merthyr Tydfil, Mid Glamorgan   CF47 8RF
Record Attendance: 21,000 (1949)
Pitch Size: 110 × 72 yards

Colours: Black and White striped shirts, Black shorts
Telephone Nº: (01685) 384102
Fax Number: (01685) 382882
Ground Capacity: 6,000
Seating Capacity: 1,500
Web Site: home.clara.net/owain/martyrs

GENERAL INFORMATION

Supporters Club: Andrew Evans, c/o Club
Telephone Nº: (01685) 384102
Car Parking: At the ground and street parking
Coach Parking: Georgetown
Nearest Railway Station: Merthyr Tydfil (½ mile)
Nearest Bus Station: Merthyr Tydfil
Club Shop: At the ground
Opening Times: Weekdays 9.00am to 4.00pm and Matchdays
Telephone Nº: (01685) 384102
Police Telephone Nº: (01685) 722541

GROUND INFORMATION

Away Supporters' Entrances & Sections:
Theatre End entrances and accommodation

ADMISSION INFO (2003/2004 PRICES)

Adult Standing: £6.00
Adult Seating: £7.00
Child Standing: £1.00   (Under 14's)
Child Seating: £2.00   (Under 14's)
Senior Citizens Standing: £4.00
Senior Citizens Seating: £5.00
Programme Price: £1.20

DISABLED INFORMATION

Wheelchairs: 20 spaces are available in total in front of the Main Grandstand
Helpers: Please phone the club for information
Prices: Please phone the club for information
Disabled Toilets: Available at the Strikers Club (Clubhouse)
Contact: (01685) 384102   (Bookings are not necessary)

Travelling Supporters' Information:
Routes: From the East: Take the A470 to Merthyr. At the top of Merthyr High Street. take a sharp left at the lights and then 1st right into Brecon Road. Take the 1st right and then 1st right once again and follow the road into the ground; From the North: Leave the A465 Heads of the Valleys road for Dowlais. After approximately 2 miles, fork right into Brecon Road. Take the 1st right then 1st right once again and follow the road into the ground.

NEWPORT COUNTY FC

Founded: 1989
Former Names: Newport AFC
Nickname: 'The Exiles'
Ground: Newport Stadium, Spytty Park, Langland Way, Newport   NP19 4PT
Record Attendance: 3,721 (28/11/2001)
Pitch Size: 112 × 72 yards

Colours: Amber shirts with Black shorts
Telephone N°: (01633) 662262
Fax Number: (01633) 666107
Ground Capacity: 4,300
Seating Capacity: 1,200
Web site: www.newport-county.co.uk
Club Call N°: (09068) 884546

GENERAL INFORMATION

Supporters Club: Bob Herrin, c/o Club
Telephone N°: (01633) 274440
Car Parking: Space for 500 cars at the ground
Coach Parking: At the ground
Nearest Railway Station: Newport
Nearest Bus Station: Newport
Club Shop: At the ground
Opening Times: Weekdays & Matchdays 10.00am–4.00pm
Telephone N°: (01633) 662262
Police Telephone N°: (01633) 244999

GROUND INFORMATION

Away Supporters' Entrances & Sections:
No segregation unless specifically required by Police

ADMISSION INFO (2003/2004 PRICES)

Adult Standing: £8.00
Adult Seating: £8.00
Senior Citizen Standing: £5.50
Senior Citizen Seating: £5.50
Child Standing: £2.50
Child Seating: £2.50
Programme Price: £1.50

DISABLED INFORMATION

Wheelchairs: Accommodated
Helpers: Admitted
Prices: Normal prices apply for disabled and helpers
Disabled Toilets: Yes
Contact: (01633) 662262   (Bookings are not necessary)

Travelling Supporters' Information:
Routes: Exit the M4 at Junction 24 and take the first exit at the roundabout, signposted 'Industrial Area'. After approximately a mile, turn left at the roundabout and then straight on at two further roundabouts before turning left and then left again into the stadium. The stadium is signposted from the M4 roundabout.

THE WELSH PREMIER LEAGUE

Address

Plymouth Chambers, 3 Westgate Street,
Cardiff   CF10 1DP

Contact   John Deakin

Phone (029) 2037-2325   **Fax** (029) 2034-3961

Clubs for the 2003/2004 Season

Aberystwyth Town FC .... Page 12

Afan Lido FC .... Page 13

Bangor City FC .... Page 14

Barry Town FC .... Page 15

Caernarfon Town FC .... Page 16

Caersws FC .... Page 17

Carmarthen Town FC .... Page 18

Connah's Quay Nomads FC .... Page 19

Cwmbran Town FC .... Page 20

Haverfordwest County FC .... Page 21

Newi Cefn Druids FC .... Page 22

Newtown AFC .... Page 23

Porthmadog FC .... Page 24

Port Talbot Town FC .... Page 25

Rhyl FC .... Page 26

Total Network Solutions FC .... Page 27

Welshpool Town FC .... Page 28

ABERYSTWYTH TOWN FC

Founded: 1884
Former Names: Aberystwyth FC
Nickname: 'Seasiders'
Ground: Park Avenue, Aberystwyth, Dyfed
Ground Telephone Nº: (01970) 612122/617939

Colours: Green and Black shirts with Black shorts
Correspondence Address: Rhun Owens, 31 Maes Gogerddan, Aberystwyth
Contact Nº: (01970) 623520 or (07773) 230894
Fax Number: (01970) 617939

GENERAL INFORMATION
Club Shop: Yes
Car Parking: Adjacent to the ground
Coach Parking: At the ground
Nearest Railway Station: Aberystwyth (¼ mile)
Nearest Bus Station: Aberystwyth (¼ mile)
Nearest Police Station: Aberystwyth
Police Telephone Nº: (01970) 612791

GROUND INFORMATION
Ground Capacity: 4,050
Seating Capacity: 550
Record Attendance: 4,000
Pitch Size: 110 x 78 yards

ADMISSION INFO (2003/2004 PRICES)
Adult Standing: £5.00
Adult Seating: £5.00
Child Standing: £2.00
Child Seating: £2.00
Note: Under 14's are admitted free of charge
Concessionary Standing: £2.00
Concessionary Seating: £2.00
Programme Price: £1.00

DISABLED SUPPORTERS INFORMATION
Wheelchairs: Accommodated in the Dias Stand
Disabled Toilets: Yes
Contact Number: (01970) 612122

Web Site: www.atfcnews.co.uk

Travelling Supporters' Information:
Routes: From the Railway Station: Turn left into Park Avenue then right after Greenfield Street and the ground is at the far end on the right behind the Bus Depot; From the East of Town: Follow the 'Town Centre' signs from the Safeway roundabout. The ground is on the left after the Kwiksave store.

AFAN LIDO FC

Founded: 1967
Former Names: None
Nickname: None
Ground: Afan Lido Football Ground, Princess Margaret Way, Port Talbot
Ground Telephone N°: (01639) 892960

Office Telephone N°: (01639) 881432
Office Fax N°: (01639) 881432
Colours: Shirts are Red with White trim, Red shorts
Correspondence Address: P. Robinson, 56 Abbeyville Avenue, Sandfields Estate, Port Talbot, SA12 6PY
Contact Telephone N°: (01639) 885638

GENERAL INFORMATION
Club Shop: Yes – at the ground
Car Parking: At the ground
Coach Parking: At the ground
Nearest Railway Station: Port Talbot Parkway
Nearest Bus Station: Port Talbot
Nearest Police Station: Sandfields, Port Talbot
Police Telephone N°: (01639) 883101

GROUND INFORMATION
Ground Capacity: 5,000
Seating Capacity: 525
Record Attendance: 1,100
Pitch Size: 112 x 75 yards

ADMISSION INFO (2003/2004 PRICES)
Adult Standing: £3.50
Adult Seating: £3.50
Child Standing: £1.00
Child Seating: £1.00
Senior Citizen Standing: £2.00
Senior Citizen Seating: £2.00
Programme Price: £1.00

DISABLED SUPPORTERS INFORMATION
Wheelchairs: Accommodated
Disabled Toilets: Available
Contact Number: (01639) 881432

Web Site: www.afanlidofc.co.uk
E-mail: afanlidofc@aol.com

Travelling Supporters' Information:
Routes: Take the M4 and exit at Junction 40. Follow all signs to Aberavon Beach from the Station – past Aberavon Centre, along Water Street, Ysgythan Road and Victoria Road, right at Afan Lido.

BANGOR CITY FC

Founded: 1876
Former Names: Bangor Athletic FC
Nickname: 'Citizens'
Ground: The Stadium, Farrar Road, Bangor, Gwynedd
Ground Telephone Nº: (01248) 355852

Club Colours: Blue shirts and shorts
Correspondence Address: Alun Griffiths, 12 Lon Y Bryn, Menai Bridge, Anglesey, Gwynedd, LL55 5NM
Contact Telephone Nº: (01248) 712820
Fax Number: (01248) 372132

GENERAL INFORMATION
Club Shop: Yes
Car Parking: Street parking and limited space at the ground
Coach Parking: By Police direction
Nearest Railway Station: Bangor (150 yards)
Nearest Bus Station: Bangor (500 yards)
Nearest Police Station: Bangor
Police Telephone Nº: (01248) 370333

GROUND INFORMATION
Ground Capacity: 1,500
Seating Capacity: 700
Record Attendance: 10,000 vs Wrexham – Welsh Cup Final 1978-79
Pitch Size: 118 x 75 yards

ADMISSION INFO (2003/2004 PRICES)
Adult Standing: £6.00
Adult Seating: £6.00
Child Standing: £3.00
Child Seating: £3.00
Concessionary Standing: £3.00
Concessionary Seating: £3.00
Programme Price: £1.00

DISABLED SUPPORTERS INFORMATION
Wheelchairs: Accommodated
Disabled Toilets: None
Contact Number: (01248) 355852

Web Site: www.bangorcityfc.com
E-mail: bangorcity@excite.co.uk

Travelling Supporters' Information:
Routes: Take the A55 Expressway to the A5 turnoff (signposted Betws-y-Coed/Bangor) and follow signs for Llandegai/Bangor. After 2½ miles pass the marina on the right and follow the road to the left. Continue for ¾ mile and the Ground is situated on Farrar Road, 150 yards from Bangor Railway Station.

BARRY TOWN FC

Founded: 1893
Former Names: None
Nickname: 'The Dragons'
Ground: Jenner Park, Barry, South Glamorgan, CF62 9BG

Social Club Telephone Nº: (01446) 735858
Club Colours: Yellow and Blue shirts, Yellow shorts
Correspondence Address: c/o Club
Contact Telephone Nº: (01446) 735858
Fax Number: (01446) 701884

GENERAL INFORMATION
Club Shop: Yes
Car Parking: At the ground
Coach Parking: At the ground
Nearest Railway Station: Barry
Nearest Bus Station: Barry
Nearest Police Station: Barry
Police Telephone Nº: (01446) 734451

GROUND INFORMATION
Ground Capacity: 2,500
Seating Capacity: 2,500
Record Attendance: Not known
Pitch Size: 105 x 75 yards

ADMISSION INFO (2003/2004 PRICES)
Adult Seating: £6.00
Child Seating: £2.00
Concessionary Seating: £4.00
Programme Price: £1.00

DISABLED SUPPORTERS INFORMATION
Wheelchairs: Accommodated
Disabled Toilets: Available
Contact Number: (01446) 721171

Travelling Supporters' Information:
Routes: Take the M4 and exit at Junction 33. Follow the A4050 to Barry for Jenner Park.

CAERNARFON TOWN FC

Founded: 1876
Former Names: Caernarfon Athletic FC, Caernarfon Ironopolis FC and Caernarfon United FC
Nickname: 'The Canaries'
Ground: The Oval, Marcus Street, Caernarfon, Gwynedd
Ground Telephone Nº: (01286) 675002

Club Colours: Yellow shirts, Green shorts
Correspondence Address: Ian Sixsmith, Caernarfon Air Park, Dynas Dinlle, Caernarfon LL54 5TP
Contact Telephone Nº: (0870) 7541500
Fax Number: (0870) 7541510

GENERAL INFORMATION
Club Shop: Yes – at the ground
Car Parking: At the ground
Coach Parking: At the ground
Nearest Railway Station: Bangor (9 miles)
Nearest Bus Station: Caernarfon (½ mile)
Nearest Police Station: Maesincla, Caernarfon
Police Telephone Nº: (01286) 673333

GROUND INFORMATION
Ground Capacity: 3,678
Seating Capacity: 252
Record Attendance: 6,000 vs Bangor City (25/12/26)
Pitch Size: 110 x 70 yards

ADMISSION INFO (2003/2004 PRICES)
Adult Standing: £5.00
Adult Seating: £5.00
Child Standing: £3.00
Child Seating: £3.00
Programme Price: £1.00

DISABLED SUPPORTERS INFORMATION
Wheelchairs: Accommodated
Disabled Toilets: None
Contact Number: (01286) 675002

Travelling Supporters' Information:
Routes: From Bangor: Travel along the A55 coast road. Ignore an "up hill" slip road which has a secondary Caernarfon signpost on a white background. Exit at a "down hill" slip road further along, signposted Caernarfon A487. Continue on the A487 into Caernarfon and staying on the A487 travel along a short flyover. At the end of the flyover, with the Eagles Hotel facing, move to the left hand lane and follow the A4085 Beddgelert Road. Travel along the A4085 almost to the brow of the hill then turn right into Segontium Road South just before the Roman Fort. The ground is facing at the bottom of the road.

CAERSWS FC

Founded: 1878
Former Names: Caersws Amateurs FC
Nickname: 'Blue Birds'
Ground: Recreation Ground, Caersws, Powys
Ground Telephone Nº: (01686) 688753

Club Colours: Blue shirts with White shorts
Correspondence: Gwilym Lewis, 1 Dolwnog,
Main Street, Caersws   SY17 5EN
Contact Telephone Nº: (01686) 688586
Fax Number: (01686) 688586

GENERAL INFORMATION
Club Shop: At the ground
Car Parking: At the ground
Coach Parking: At the ground
Nearest Railway Station: Caersws (¼ mile)
Nearest Bus Station: Newtown
Nearest Police Station: Llanidloes
Police Telephone Nº: (01686) 412222

GROUND INFORMATION
Ground Capacity: 3,000
Seating Capacity: 150
Record Attendance: 2,656
Pitch Size: 110 x 70 yards

ADMISSION INFO (2003/2004 PRICES)
Adult Standing: £4.00
Adult Seating: £4.00
Senior Citizen/Child Standing: £2.00
Senior Citizen/Child Seating: £2.00
Programme Price: £1.00

DISABLED SUPPORTERS INFORMATION
Wheelchairs: Accommodated
Disabled Toilets: Available
Contact Number: (01686) 688753

Web Site: www.caersws-fc.com

Travelling Supporters' Information:
Routes: The entrance to the ground is by the River Bridge in Caersws. Caersws is situated on the A470 between Newtown and Llanidloes.

CARMARTHEN TOWN FC

Founded: 1953
Former Names: None
Nickname: 'Town'
Ground: Richmond Park, Priory Street, Carmarthen, Carmarthenshire
Club Office Nº: (01267) 222851

Clubhouse Nº: (01267) 232101
Club Colours: Old Gold shirts with Black shorts
Correspondence Address: G.O. Jones, Carmarthen Town, 131 Priory Street, Carmarthen SA31 1LR
Contact Telephone Nº: (01267) 233359
Fax Number: (01267) 222851

GENERAL INFORMATION
Club Shop: Yes – at the ground
Car Parking: Adjacent to the ground
Coach Parking: Adjacent to the ground
Nearest Railway Station: Carmarthen (1 mile)
Nearest Bus Station: Blue Street, Carmarthen
Nearest Police Station: Carmarthen
Police Telephone Nº: (01267) 232000

GROUND INFORMATION
Ground Capacity: 2,000
Seating Capacity: 500
Record Attendance: 3,000
Pitch Size: 110 x 70 yards

ADMISSION INFO (2003/2004 PRICES)
Adult Standing: £4.00
Adult Seating: £4.00
Child Standing: £2.00
Child Seating: £2.00
Note: Children under 11 are admitted free of charge
Programme Price: £1.00

DISABLED SUPPORTERS INFORMATION
Wheelchairs: Accommodated
Disabled Toilets: None – but adapted toilet available
Contact Number: (01267) 232101

Web Site: www.carmarthentownafc.net
E-mail: info@carmarthentownafc.net

Travelling Supporters' Information:
Routes: Proceed into Carmarthen on the A48. Pick up the A40 to Llandeilo at the first roundabout and follow the Town Centre sign at the next roundabout. The ground is situated on the left hand side in Priory Street, behind the Toyota Garage.

CONNAH'S QUAY NOMADS FC

Founded: 1946
Former Names: Connah's Quay Juniors FC
Nickname: 'Westenders'
Ground: Deeside College, Kelsterton Road,
Connah's Quay, Flintshire   CH5 4LU
Ground Telephone N°: (01244) 816418

Club Colours: White shirts with Black shorts
Correspondence Address: R. Hunter,
40 Brookdale Avenue, Connah's Quay   CH5 4LU
Contact Telephone N°: (01244) 831212
Fax Number: (01244) 831212

GENERAL INFORMATION
Club Shop: Yes
Car Parking: Street parking
Coach Parking: At the ground
Nearest Railway Station: Shotton (1 mile)
Nearest Bus Station: Flint (2 miles)
Nearest Police Station: Wepre Drive, Connah's Quay
Police Telephone N°: (01244) 814444

GROUND INFORMATION
Ground Capacity: 3,000
Seating Capacity: 500
Record Attendance: Approximately 850
Pitch Size: 110 x 70 yards

ADMISSION INFO (2003/2004 PRICES)
Adult Standing: £5.00
Adult Seating: £5.00
Child Standing: £1.50
Child Seating: £1.50
Concessionary Standing: £1.50
Concessionary Seating: £1.50
Programme Price: £1.00

DISABLED SUPPORTERS INFORMATION
Wheelchairs: Accommodated
Disabled Toilets: Available
Contact Number: (01244) 816418

Travelling Supporters' Information:
Routes: The ground is situated on the main A548 road through Connah's Quay in the grounds of Deeside College.

CWMBRAN TOWN FC

Founded: 1950
Former Names: None
Nickname: 'The Town'
Ground: Cwmbran Stadium, Henllys Way, Cwmbran, Gwent
Ground Telephone Nº: (01633) 627100

Club Colours: Dark Blue shirts and shorts
Correspondence Address: R.L. Langley, 77 Hampton Crescent East, Cyncoed, Cardiff, CF23 6RG
Contact Telephone Nº: (029) 2076-4381
Fax Number: (029) 2076-4381

GENERAL INFORMATION
Social Club Telephone Nº: (01633) 483282
Club Shop: Yes
Car Parking: At the ground
Coach Parking: At the ground
Nearest Railway Station: Cwmbran (2 miles)
Nearest Bus Station: Cwmbran (1 mile)
Nearest Police Station: Cwmbran (1 mile)
Police Telephone Nº: (01633) 838999

GROUND INFORMATION
Ground Capacity: 8,201
Seating Capacity: 3,000
Record Attendance: 8,148 vs Manchester United (1994)
Pitch Size: 112 x 76 yards

ADMISSION INFO (2003/2004 PRICES)
Adult Standing: £5.00
Adult Seating: £5.00
Child Standing: £3.00
Child Seating: £3.00
Concessionary Standing: £3.00
Concessionary Seating: £3.00
Programme Price: £1.00

DISABLED SUPPORTERS INFORMATION
Wheelchairs: Accommodated
Disabled Toilets: Available
Contact Number: (01633) 627100

Web Site: www.cwmbrantownafc.co.uk
E-mail: roy.langley@virgin.net

Travelling Supporters' Information:
Routes: From All Parts: Take the M4, exit at Junction 26 and follow signs for Cwmbran. At the first roundabout (approximately 1½ to 2 miles) take the first exit. Proceed along Cwmbran Drive passing the Stadium on your right. At the next roundabout take the first exit and at the following roundabout take the 3rd exit. The Stadium entrance is 150 yards on the right.
On foot from the station – proceed to the dual carriageway, turn left and Henllys Way is on the right after 1 mile.

HAVERFORDWEST COUNTY FC

Founded: 1899
Former Names: None
Nickname: 'The Bluebirds'
Ground: The Bridge Meadow Stadium, Haverfordwest, Pembrokeshire   SA61 2EX
Ground Telephone Nº: (01437) 769048

Club Colours: Blue shirts and shorts
Correspondence Address: c/o Club
Contact Telephone Nº: (01437) 731779
Fax Number: (01437) 769048

GENERAL INFORMATION
Social Club Telephone Nº: (01437) 769048
Club Shop: Yes – at the ground
Car Parking: At the ground
Coach Parking: At the ground
Nearest Railway Station: Haverfordwest (½ mile)
Nearest Bus Station: Haverfordwest
Nearest Police Station: Haverfordwest
Police Telephone Nº: (01437) 763355

GROUND INFORMATION
Ground Capacity: 2,000
Seating Capacity: 400
Record Attendance: Not known
Pitch Size: 110 x 75 yards

ADMISSION INFO (2003/2004 PRICES)
Adult Standing: £4.00
Adult Seating: £4.00
Child Standing: £2.00
Child Seating: £2.00
Concessionary Standing: £2.00
Concessionary Seating: £2.00
Programme Price: £1.00

DISABLED SUPPORTERS INFORMATION
Wheelchairs: Accommodated
Disabled Toilets: Available
Contact Number: (01437) 731779

Web Site: www.haverfordwestcounty.com
E-mail: barryvaughan3@aol.com

Travelling Supporters' Information:
Routes: Take the A40 to Haverfordwest and into the Town Centre. Pass the Railway Station, take the 4th exit at the roundabout and the take the 1st exit at the next roundabout. At the following roundabout, take the 'Safeways' exit and turn left alongside Safeways Supermarket. The ground is situated at the end of the road.

NEWI CEFN DRUIDS FC

Founded: 1992 with the amalgamation of Cefn Albion FC and Druids United FC
Former Names: Cefn Druids FC, Flexsys Cefn Druids FC
Nickname: 'The Ancients'
Ground: Plaskynaston Lane, Cefn Mawr, Wrexham, LL14 3AT
Ground Telelephone N°: (01978) 824279

Club Colours: Black & White striped shirts with Black shorts
Correspondence Address: Awelon, Copperas Hill, Penycae, Wrexham   LL14 2SA
Contact Telephone N°: (01978) 845988
Fax Number: (01878) 824332

GENERAL INFORMATION
Club Shop: At the ground
Car Parking: At the ground
Coach Parking: At the ground
Nearest Railway Station: Ruabon
Nearest Bus Station: Wrexham
Nearest Police Station: Ruabon
Police Telephone N°: (01978) 290222

GROUND INFORMATION
Ground Capacity: 2,000
Seating Capacity: 300
Record Attendance: 602
Pitch Size: 110 x 72 yards

ADMISSION INFO (2003/2004 PRICES)
Adult Standing: £5.00
Adult Seating: £5.00
Child Standing: £1.00
Child Seating: £1.00
Concessionary Standing: £3.00
Concessionary Seating: £3.00
Programme Price: £1.00

DISABLED SUPPORTERS INFORMATION
Wheelchairs: Accommodated
Disabled Toilets: Available
Contact Number: (01978) 845988

Web Site: www.cefndruids.co.uk

Travelling Supporters' Information:
Routes: From All Parts: Take the A483 and Wrexham Bypass to the junction with the A539 then turn left towards Rhosmedre on the B5605. Turn right at the Plough Inn towards Cefn Mawr and after the Kwiksave supermarket turn left down the narrow lane to the ground.

NEWTOWN AFC

Founded: 1875
Former Names: Newtown Whitestars FC
Nickname: 'The Robins'
Ground: Latham Park, Newtown, Powys
Ground Telephone Nº: (01686) 623120

Club Colours: Red shirts and shorts
Correspondence: c/o Club
Contact Telephone Nº: (01686) 623120
Fax Number: (01686) 623813
Web Site: www.newtownafc.co.uk
E-mail: office@newtownafc.co.uk

GENERAL INFORMATION
Club Shop: Yes – at the ground
Car Parking: At the ground
Coach Parking: At the ground
Nearest Railway Station: Newtown
Nearest Bus Station: Newtown Back Lane
Nearest Police Station: Newtown
Police Telephone Nº: (01686) 622777

GROUND INFORMATION
Ground Capacity: 4,999
Seating Capacity: 1,780
Record Attendance: 5,004 vs Swansea (1955)
Pitch Size: 112 x 72 yards

ADMISSION INFO (2003/2004 PRICES)
Adult Seating: £6.00 (Members £4.00)
Child Seating: £3.00
Concessionary Seating: £3.00
Programme Price: £1.00

DISABLED SUPPORTERS INFORMATION
Wheelchairs: Accommodated
Disabled Toilets: Available
Contact Number: (01686) 623120

Travelling Supporters' Information:
Routes: The ground is situated on the fringe of the Town Centre, just next to the junction of the A483 and A489 behind the Police Station. Turn into Park Lane from Park Street by the Town Library. Latham Park is 400 yards along Park Lane on the left.

PORTHMADOG FC

Founded: 1884
Former Names: None
Nickname: 'Port'
Ground: Y Traeth, Porthmadog, Gwynedd
Ground Telephone Nº: (01766) 514687

Club Colours: Red & Black striped shirts, Black shorts
Correspondence: H. Merrion Parry, 19 Pensyflog, Porthmadog LL49 9LP
Contact Telephone Nº: (01766) 512353
Fax Number: (01766) 512991

GENERAL INFORMATION

Club Shop: Yes – at the ground
Car Parking: At the ground
Coach Parking: At the ground
Nearest Railway Station: Porthmadog (½ mile)
Nearest Bus Station: Porthmadog (½ mile)
Nearest Police Station: Porthmadog
Police Telephone Nº: (01766) 512226

GROUND INFORMATION

Ground Capacity: 4,000
Seating Capacity: 500
Record Attendance: 3,500
Pitch Size: 116 x 76 yards

ADMISSION INFO (2003/2004 PRICES)

Adult Standing: £4.00
Adult Seating: £4.00
Child Standing: £3.00 (Accompanied by an adult only)
Child Seating: £3.00 (Accompanied by an adult only)
Senior Citizen Standing: £2.00
Senior Citizen Seating: £2.00
Programme Price: £1.00

DISABLED SUPPORTERS INFORMATION

Wheelchairs: Accommodated
Disabled Toilets: Available
Contact Number: (01766) 514687

Travelling Supporters' Information:
Routes: At the crossroads in the town (by Woolworths), go down Snowdon Street, cross over Madog Street and pass the British Legion Club and Porthmadog Pottery Workshop. Carry on over the railway crossing and the ground is situated on the right; Alternative Route: Turn at the side of the British Rail and West Highland Railway Stations into Cambrian Terrace and continue for ½ mile then turn at the fish and chip shop past the Porthmadog Pottery. Then as above.

PORT TALBOT TOWN FC

Founded: 1901
Former Names: Port Talbot Athletic FC
Nickname: 'The Blues'
Ground: Victoria Road Ground, Victoria Road,
Port Talbot   SA12 6AD
Ground Telephone Nº: (01639) 882465

Colours: Blue shirts and shorts
Correspondence: Paul Fisher, 87 Village Gardens,
Port Talbot   SA12 7LP
Contact Telephone Nº: (01639) 793689
Fax Number: (01639) 886991
Web Site: www.porttalbotafc.co.uk
E-mail: p.fisher2@ntlworld.com

GENERAL INFORMATION
Social Club Telephone Nº: (01639) 882465
Club Shop: Yes
Car Parking: Street parking
Coach Parking: At the ground
Nearest Railway Station: Port Talbot Parkway (2 miles)
Nearest Bus Station: Port Talbot Centre
Nearest Police Station: Station Road, Port Talbot
Police Telephone Nº: (01639) 883101

GROUND INFORMATION
Ground Capacity: 780
Seating Capacity: 280
Record Attendance: Over 2,000
Pitch Size: 118 x 70 yards

ADMISSION INFO (2003/2003 PRICES)
Adult Standing: £4.00
Adult Seating: £4.00
Child Standing: £2.00
Child Seating: £2.00
Concessionary Standing: £2.00
Concessionary Seating: £2.00
Programme Price: £1.00

DISABLED SUPPORTERS INFORMATION
Wheelchairs: Accommodated
Disabled Toilets: Available in the Clubhouse
Contact Number: (01639) 882465

Travelling Supporters' Information:
Routes: Exit the M4 at Junction 40 and head for the Town Centre. Bear left at the first roundabout for Aberavon beach and turn right at the traffic lights at the Health Centre into Victoria Road. Turn 2nd left after the traffic lights for the ground.

RHYL FC

Founded: 1870
Former Names: Rhyl Skull & Crossbones FC and Rhyl Athletic FC
Nickname: 'Lilywhites'
Ground: Belle Vue, Grange Road, Rhyl, Flintshire
Ground Telephone N°: (01745) 338327

Club Colours: White shirts with Black shorts
Correspondence Address: Dennis McNamee, 3 Maes Rhoslyn, Rhuddlan LL18 2YW
Contact Telephone N°: (01745) 591287
Fax Number: (01745) 338327
Web Site: www.rhylfc.com
E-mail: admin@rhylfc.com

GENERAL INFORMATION
Club Shop: Yes – at the ground
Car Parking: At the ground
Coach Parking: At the ground
Nearest Railway Station: Rhyl
Nearest Bus Station: Rhyl Town Centre
Nearest Police Station: Rhyl
Police Telephone N°: (01745) 343898

GROUND INFORMATION
Ground Capacity: 3,800
Seating Capacity: 300
Record Attendance: 10,000 vs Cardiff City (1952/53)
Pitch Size: 110 x 75 yards

ADMISSION INFO (2003/2004 PRICES)
Adult Standing: £6.00
Adult Seating: £6.00
Child Standing: £1.00
Child Seating: £1.00
Concessionary Standing: £4.00
Concessionary Seating: £4.00
Programme Price: £1.00

DISABLED SUPPORTERS INFORMATION
Wheelchairs: Accommodated
Disabled Toilets: Available
Contact Number: (01745) 338327

Travelling Supporters' Information:
Routes: Take the A55 Expressway and exit at the St. Asaph/Rhyl turn-off. Take the A525 to Rhuddlan. At the roundabout, take the second turning for Rhyl, turn left at the next roundabout and then travel straight on at the next two roundabouts. At the Shell garage, situated about a mile from the last roundabout, turn right along Pendyffryn Road and then left at the junction. The ground is 300 yards on the left.

TOTAL NETWORK SOLUTIONS FC

Founded: 1959
Former Names: Llansantffraid FC
The club amalgamated with Oswestry Town in 2003.
Nickname: 'Saints'
Ground: Recreation Ground, Treflan, Llansantffraid, Powys
Ground Telephone Nº: (01691) 828112

Club Colours: Green and white Hooped shirts with White shorts *or* Royal Blue shirts and shorts
Correspondence Address: G. Hughes, Birchlea, Porthywaen, Oswestry   SY10 8LY
Contact Telephone/Fax Nº: (01691) 828645
Web Site: www.tnsfc.co.uk
E-mail: richard.hann@tns.co.uk

GENERAL INFORMATION
Club Shop: None
Car Parking: At the ground
Coach Parking: At the ground
Nearest Railway Station: Gobowen & Welshpool
Nearest Bus Station: Oswestry
Nearest Police Station: Llanfyllin
Police Telephone Nº: (01691) 648222

GROUND INFORMATION
Ground Capacity: 2,000
Seating Capacity: 500
Record Attendance: Approximately 2,000
Pitch Size: 110 x 75 yards

ADMISSION INFO (2003/2004 PRICES)
Adult Standing: £4.00
Adult Seating: £4.00
Child Standing: £1.00
Child Seating: £1.00
Senior Citizen Standing: £2.00
Senior Citizen Seating: £2.00
Programme Price: £1.00

DISABLED SUPPORTERS INFORMATION
Wheelchairs: Accommodated
Disabled Toilets: Available
Contact Number: (01691) 828645

Travelling Supporters' Information:
Routes: From the South: Take the B4393 of the A483 Welshpool to Oswestry Road at 'Four Crosses' and head into Llansantffraid. The ground is situated in the centre of the village opposite Wynnstay Farmers Mill. Turn right and the ground is along the road next to the Community Hall; From the North: Take the A483 from Oswestry and turn right onto the A495 at Llynclys. Follow the road to Llansantffraid then as from the South.

WELSHPOOL TOWN FC

Founded: 1878
Former Names: None
Nickname: 'Lilywhites'
Ground: Maesydre, Welshpool, Powys
Ground Telephone N°: None

Club Colours: White shirts with Black shorts
Correspondence Address: Mike Edwards,
2 Chelsea Villas, Chelsea Lane, Welshpool, SY21 7JT
Contact Telephone N°: (01938) 555140
Fax Number: (01938) 555855

GENERAL INFORMATION
Club Shop: None
Car Parking: At the ground
Coach Parking: At the ground
Nearest Railway Station: Welshpool (2 minutes walk)
Nearest Bus Station: Welshpool (5 minutes walk)
Nearest Police Station: Welshpool
Police Telephone N°: (01938) 552345

GROUND INFORMATION
Ground Capacity: 1,500
Seating Capacity: 250
Record Attendance: Not known
Pitch Size: 108 x 72 yards

ADMISSION INFO (2003/2004 PRICES)
Adult Standing: £4.00
Adult Seating: £4.00
Child Standing: £2.00
Child Seating: £2.00
Concessionary Standing: £2.00
Concessionary Seating: £2.00
Programme Price: £1.00

DISABLED SUPPORTERS INFORMATION
Wheelchairs: Accommodated
Disabled Toilets: None
Contact Number: (01938) 555140

Travelling Supporters' Information:
Routes: The ground is situated on the south side of Welshpool Town Centre. Follow the signs for the Railway Station and turn right just before the station into Howell Drive. The ground is along the lane next to the Junior School.

CYMRU ALLIANCE FOOTBALL LEAGUE

Address

J. Alun Foulkes, 9 Brynteg Estate, Llandegfan, Menai Bridge, Ynys Mon   LL59 5TY

Phone (01248) 713501   **Fax** (01248) 714644

Clubs for the 2003/2004 Season

Airbus UK FC .... Page 30

Amlwch FC .... Page 31

Buckley Town FC .... Page 32

Cemaes Bay FC .... Page 33

Flint Town United FC .... Page 34

Glantraeth FC .... Page 35

Gresford Athletic FC .... Page 36

Guilsfield FC .... Page 37

Halkyn United FC .... Page 38

Holyhead Hotspur FC.. Page 39

Holywell Town FC.. Page 40

Lex XI FC .... Page 41

Llandudno FC .... Page 42

Llanfairpwll FC .... Page 43

Llangefni Town FC... Page 44

Mold Alexandra FC .... Page 45

Ruthin Town FC .... Page 46

AIRBUS UK FC

Founded: –
Former Names: British Aerospace FC
Nickname: 'Planemakers'
Ground: Sports & Social Club, BAE System Airbus UK, Broughton, Chester   CH4 0DR
Ground Telephone Nº: (01244) 522393

Club Colours: Dark Blue shirts and shorts
Correspondence: Terry Melia, 17 Salisbury Avenue, Saltney, Chester   CH4 8TF
Contact Telephone Nº: (01244) 680446
Fax Number: None

GENERAL INFORMATION
Club Shop: None
Car Parking: By the Main Gates
Coach Parking: By the Main Gates
Nearest Railway Station: Shotton (5 miles)
Nearest Bus Station: Chester (5 miles)
Nearest Police Station: Hawarden
Police Telephone Nº: –

GROUND INFORMATION
Ground Capacity: 1,000
Seating Capacity: 75
Record Attendance: 340
Pitch Size: 110 x 75 yards

ADMISSION INFO (2003/2004 PRICES)
Adult Standing: £2.00
Adult Seating: £2.00
Child Standing: £1.00
Child Seating: £1.00
Programme Price: Included with admission

DISABLED SUPPORTERS INFORMATION
Wheelchairs: Accommodated
Disabled Toilets: Available in the Social Club
Contact Number: (01244) 522393

Travelling Supporters' Information:
Routes: Exit the A55 Expressway at the Broughton turn-off and follow signs for the Aerospace Factory. Park at the Main Gates where directions to the ground will be given.

AMLWCH FC

Founded: 1897
Former Names: None
Nickname: 'Town' 'The Blues'
Ground: Lon Bach, Amlwch, Anglesey   LL68 9BL
Ground Telephone Nº: None

Club Colours: Royal Blue shirts and shorts
Correspondence Address: Alan Strawson,
20 Chapel Street, Amlwch Port, Amlwch   LL68 9HT
Contact Telephone Nº: (01407) 831696
Fax Number: None
Web Site: www.amlwchtownfc.co.uk
E-mail: alan@astrawson.fsnet.co.uk

GENERAL INFORMATION
Club Shop: At the ground
Car Parking: At the ground
Coach Parking: At the ground
Nearest Railway Station: Bangor or Holyhead (20 miles)
Nearest Bus Station: Amlwch
Nearest Police Station: Amlwch
Police Telephone Nº: (01407) 830222

GROUND INFORMATION
Ground Capacity: 1,000
Seating Capacity: 70
Record Attendance: Not known
Pitch Size: 110 x 70 yards

ADMISSION INFO (2003/2004 PRICES)
Adult Standing: £3.00 (by programme)
Adult Seating: £3.00 (by programme)
Child Standing: Free of charge
Child Seating: Free of charge
Programme Price: Included in admission price

DISABLED SUPPORTERS INFORMATION
Wheelchairs: Accommodated
Disabled Toilets: Available
Contact Number: (01407) 831696

Travelling Supporters' Information:
Routes: Take the A55/A5 to Anglesey across the Menai Bridge then take the 2nd slip road (A5025) marked Amlwch (Amlwch is about 18 miles). On entering Amlwch, continue across the roundabout and after a third of a mile turn left onto Mona Street (after the Total Garage). Continue for ¼ mile and turn right opposite the Fire Station into Lon Bach for the ground which is on the right.

BUCKLEY TOWN FC

Founded: 1948
Former Names: Fomed by the amalgamation of Buckley Wanderers FC and Buckley Rovers FC in 1978
Nickname: 'Wanderers'
Ground: Globe Way, Liverpool Road, Buckley, Flintshire
Ground Tel. Nº: (07803) 137523

Club Colours: Red and White shirts with Red shorts
Correspondence: Michael Williams,
4 Hillary Grove, Buckley, Flintshire
Contact Telephone Nº: (01244) 546893
Fax Number: None

GENERAL INFORMATION
Club Shop: None
Car Parking: At the ground
Coach Parking: At the ground
Nearest Railway Station: Buckley (1 mile)
Nearest Bus Station: Buckley
Nearest Police Station: Buckley
Police Telephone Nº: –

GROUND INFORMATION
Ground Capacity: 1,000
Seating Capacity: 80
Record Attendance: Approximately 750
Pitch Size: 120 x 85 yards

ADMISSION INFO (2003/2004 PRICES)
Adult Standing: £3.00
Adult Seating: £3.00
Child Standing: £1.00
Child Seating: £1.00
Programme Price: £1.00

DISABLED SUPPORTERS INFORMATION
Wheelchairs: Accommodated
Disabled Toilets: Available
Contact Number: (01244) 546893

Travelling Supporters' Information:
Routes: Exit the A55 Expressway at its junction with the A550 following signs for Buckley. Pass through Ewloe village and head towards Buckley. As the road reaches the outskirts of Buckley (about 300 yards from Ewloe) turn left at the Red Lion Public House into Globe Way and the ground is about ¼ mile on the right.

CEMAES BAY FC

Founded: 1976
Former Names: None
Nickname: None
Ground: School Lane Stadium, Cemaes Bay, Anglesey, Gwynedd
Ground Telephone Nº: (01407) 710600

Colours: Red shirts and shorts
Correspondence: Edryd Jones, 13 Neuadd yr Eglwys, Glynne Road, Bangor LL57 1AH
Contact Telephone Nº: (07887) 926013
Fax Number: None
E-mail: edryd.jones@dpconline.com

GENERAL INFORMATION

Club Shop: Yes – at the ground
Car Parking: At the ground
Coach Parking: At the ground
Nearest Railway Station: Valley (8 miles)
Nearest Bus Station: Amlwch (3 miles)
Nearest Police Station: Cemaes Bay
Police Telephone Nº: (01407) 710222

GROUND INFORMATION

Ground Capacity: 3,000
Seating Capacity: 310
Record Attendance: Approximately 1,500
Pitch Size: 110 x 72 yards

ADMISSION INFO (2003/2004 PRICES)

Adult Standing: £2.00
Adult Seating: £2.00
Child Standing: Free of charge
Child Seating: Free of charge
Concessionary Standing: £1.00
Concessionary Seating: £1.00
Programme Price: 50p

DISABLED SUPPORTERS INFORMATION

Wheelchairs: Accommodated
Disabled Toilets: Available
Contact Number: (01407) 710600

Travelling Supporters' Information:
Routes: Take the A55 expressway to Holyhead and exit at the 'Valley' turn-off onto the A5025. After about 9 miles, pass the turn-off for the Wylfa Nuclear Power Station and continue to the roundabout in Cemaes. Turn right at the roundabout for Llanfechell and after 100 yards turn left opposite Police House. The ground is down the track between the houses.

FLINT TOWN UNITED FC

Founded: 1886
Former Names: Flint Town FC and Flint FC
Nickname: 'Silkmen'
Ground: Cae-y-Castell, Marsh Lane, Flint, Delyn, Flintshire
Ground Telephone Nº: (01352) 730982

Colours: Black and White shirts with Black shorts
Correspondence Address: A. Baines, 43 Third Avenue, Flint CH6 5LT
Contact Telephone Nº: (01352) 731488
Fax Number: None

GENERAL INFORMATION
Social Club Telephone Nº: (01352) 732804
Club Shop: Yes – at the ground
Car Parking: At the ground
Coach Parking: At the ground
Nearest Railway Station: Flint (500 yards)
Nearest Bus Station: Flint
Nearest Police Station: Flint
Police Telephone Nº: (01352) 732222

GROUND INFORMATION
Ground Capacity: 3,000
Seating Capacity: 270
Record Attendance: 1,500 vs Wrexham (1994)
Pitch Size: 110 x 75 yards

ADMISSION INFO (2003/2004 PRICES)
Adult Standing: £3.00
Adult Seating: £3.00
Child Standing: £1.50
Child Seating: £1.50
Concessionary Standing: £1.50
Concessionary Seating: £1.50
Programme Price: £1.00

DISABLED SUPPORTERS INFORMATION
Wheelchairs: Accommodated
Disabled Toilets: Available
Contact Number: (01352) 730982

Travelling Supporters' Information:
Routes: Take the A458 from Connah's Quay into Flint and turn right opposite the Swan Hotel into Castle Street following the 'Castle' signs. Cross over the railway and the Clubhouse is next to the Lifeguard Station. The ground is along the shoreline opposite the Castle; Alternatively: Take the A55 Expressway and turn off at the Flint sign (A5119) following the road into the town. Turn right at the bottom of High Street and then left opposite the Swan Hotel over the railway to the Clubhouse and ground.

GLANTRAETH FC

Founded: 1984
Former Names: Llangefni/Glantraeth FC
Nickname: None
Ground: Trefdraeth, Bodorgan, Anglesey
Ground Telephone Nº: (01407) 840401
Club Colours: Red shirts and shorts

Correspondence Address: John Owen, Gallt Ysw, Bethel, Bodorgan LL62 5NL
Contact Telephone Nº: (01407) 840179
Fax Number: None

GENERAL INFORMATION
Club Shop: None
Car Parking: At the ground
Coach Parking: At the ground
Nearest Railway Station: Bodorgan (2 miles)
Nearest Bus Station: Llangefni (6 miles)
Nearest Police Station: Llangefni (6 miles)
Police Telephone Nº: (01248) 722222

GROUND INFORMATION
Ground Capacity: 1,500
Seating Capacity: 75
Record Attendance: Not known
Pitch Size: 110 x 72 yards

ADMISSION INFO (2003/2004 PRICES)
Adult Standing: £2.00
Adult Seating: £2.00
Child Standing: £1.00
Child Seating: £1.00
Programme Price: Included in the admission price

DISABLED SUPPORTERS INFORMATION
Wheelchairs: Accommodated
Disabled Toilets: None
Contact Number: (01407) 840401

Travelling Supporters' Information:
Routes: Exit the A55 Expressway at the Llangefni turnoff and take the A5 signposted for Mona at the roundabout. After about ¾ mile take the B4422 signposted for Aberffraw. Follow this road for 3 miles then turn left at the village of Bethel following the sign for the Glantraeth Restaurant. The ground is situated 1 mile along this road on the right-hand side.

GRESFORD ATHLETIC FC

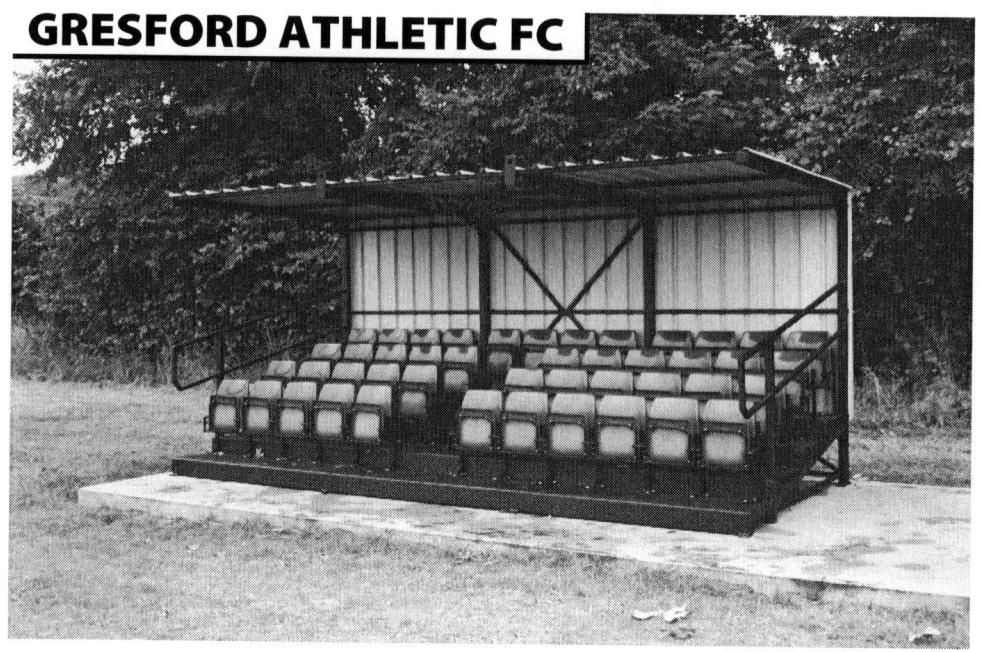

Founded: 1946
Former Names: None
Nickname: 'Athletic'
Ground: Clappers Lane, Gresford, Wrexham
Ground Telephone Nº: None
Web Site: www.gresfordathleticfc.co.uk
E-mail: chas@gresfordath.freeserve.co.uk

Colours: Shirts are Red with Black and White trim, Black shorts
Correspondence: D.C.Rowland, 26 Gorse Crescent, Marford, Near Wrexham, LL12 8LZ
Contact Telephone Nº: (01978) 855354
Fax Number: (01978) 855354

GENERAL INFORMATION
Club Shop: None
Car Parking: At the ground
Coach Parking: At the ground
Nearest Railway Station: Wrexham (4 miles)
Nearest Bus Station: Wrexham
Nearest Police Station: Wrexham
Police Telephone Nº: (01978) 290211

GROUND INFORMATION
Ground Capacity: 1,000
Seating Capacity: 60
Record Attendance: 300 (approximately)
Pitch Size: 110 x 72 yards

ADMISSION INFO (2003/2004 PRICES)
Adult Standing: £2.00 (includes programme)
Adult Seating: £2.00 (includes programme)
Child Standing: £1.00 (includes programme)
Child Seating: £1.00 (includes programme)
Programme Price: £1.00

DISABLED SUPPORTERS INFORMATION
Wheelchairs: Accommodated
Disabled Toilets: Yes
Contact Number: (01978) 855354

Travelling Supporters' Information:
Routes: Leave the A483 at the Rossett roundabout (B5102) heading towards Rossett. At the next roundabout turn right onto the B5445 and follow the road through Marford into Gresford. Turn right at the Plough Inn into the High Street then left before the Village Pond to the Village Memorial Hall for the ground.

GUILSFIELD FC

Founded: 1957
Former Names: None
Nickname: 'Gills'
Ground: The Community Ground,
The Community Centre, Guilsfield, Powys, SY21 9ND
Ground Telephone Nº: None

Colours: Red and Black shirts with Black shorts
Correspondence: G. Davies, 27 Acrefield Avenue,
Guilsfield, Welshpool SY21 9DF
Contact Telephone Nº: (01938) 554537
Fax Number: None
Web Site: www.guilsfield-fc.freeserve.co.uk
E-mail: gvl@celynlane.freeserve.co.uk

GENERAL INFORMATION
Club Shop: None
Car Parking: At the ground
Coach Parking: At the ground
Nearest Railway Station: Welshpool (3 miles)
Nearest Bus Station: Oswestry
Nearest Police Station: Welshpool
Police Telephone Nº: (01938) 552345

GROUND INFORMATION
Ground Capacity: 1,000
Seating Capacity: 55
Record Attendance: Not known
Pitch Size: 115 x 75 yards

ADMISSION INFO (2003/2004 PRICES)
Adult Standing: £2.00
Adult Seating: £2.00
Child Standing: Free of charge for Under 16s
Child Seating: Free of charge for Under 16s
Concessionary Standing: £1.00
Concessionary Seating: £1.00
Programme Price: £1.00

DISABLED SUPPORTERS INFORMATION
Wheelchairs: Accommodated
Disabled Toilets: None
Contact Number: (01938) 554537

Travelling Supporters' Information:
Routes: Take the A490 from Welshpool and the first turn-off on the right into Guilsfield. The ground is situated on the left next to the School, directly at the side of Welshpool Road.

HALKYN UNITED FC

Founded: 1945
Former Names: Halykn Rangers FC
Nickname: None
Ground: Pant Newydd, Halkyn Cricket Club, Halkyn Road, Pentre Halkyn, Flintshire
Ground Telephone Nº: (01352) 780576

Colours: Blue shirts and shorts
Correspondence Address: Brian Pugh, 7 Hafan Deg, Holway, Holywell   CH8 7DB
Contact Tel. Nº: (01352) 710431
Fax Number: (01352) 710431
Web Site: www.halkynunitedfc.co.uk

GENERAL INFORMATION
Social Club Telephone Nº: (01352) 780576
Club Shop: None
Car Parking: At the ground
Coach Parking: At the ground
Nearest Railway Station: Flint (6 miles)
Nearest Bus Station: Mold
Nearest Police Station: Colwyn Bay
Police Telephone Nº: (01352) 752321

GROUND INFORMATION
Ground Capacity: 1,000
Seating Capacity: 75
Record Attendance: 183 (vs Caerleon, February 2000)
Pitch Size: 110 x 75 yards

ADMISSION INFO (2003/2004 PRICES)
Adult Standing: £3.00 (includes programme)
Adult Seating: £3.00 (includes programme)
Child Standing: £1.00
Child Seating: £1.00
Senior Citizen Standing: £2.00 (includes programme)
Senior Citizen Seating: £2.00 (includes programme)
Programme Price: 50p

DISABLED SUPPORTERS INFORMATION
Wheelchairs: Accommodated
Disabled Toilets: Available
Contact Number: (01352) 780576

Travelling Supporters' Information:
Routes: From Chester: Take the A55 to the turn-off for Rhosemor (B5123) and turn left at Springfield Hotel to the top of the hill. Bear left and approximately ½ mile along after the double bend, the entrance gates to the Cricket Club are on the left opposite the entrance to Halkyn Hall; From Conwy: Take the A55 to the Rhosemor (B5123) turn-off and turn right at the junction. After 200 yards turn right before the Haven Garage under the A55 and continue along to the Springfield Hotel. Then as above.

HOLYHEAD HOTSPUR FC

Founded: 1990
Former Names: None
Nickname: None
Ground: New Oval, Leisure Centre, Kingsland, Holyhead, Anglesey
Ground Telephone Nº: (01407) 764111

Club Colours: Blue and White striped shirts with Black shorts
Correspondence Address: Mr R. Parry, 27 Tan y Bryn Road, Holyhead   LL65 1AR
Contact Telephone Nº: (01407) 762904
Alternative Contact: Gareth Davies (01407) 760576
Web site: www.holyhead.com/holyheadhotspur

GENERAL INFORMATION
Club Shop: At the ground
Car Parking: At the ground
Coach Parking: At the ground
Nearest Railway Station: Holyhead (½ mile)
Nearest Bus Station: Holyhead (½ mile)
Nearest Police Station: Holyhead
Police Telephone Nº: (01407) 762323

GROUND INFORMATION
Ground Capacity: 1,500
Seating Capacity: 75
Record Attendance: 1,200
Pitch Size: 110 x 75 yards

ADMISSION INFO (2003/2004 PRICES)
Adult Standing: £2.50
Adult Seating: £2.50
Child Standing: £1.50
Child Seating: £1.50
Programme Price: 60p

DISABLED SUPPORTERS INFORMATION
Wheelchairs: Accommodated
Disabled Toilets: Available
Contact Number: (01407) 764111

Travelling Supporters' Information:
Routes: Take the A55 dual carriageway into Holyhead, turn left at the first roundabout onto the B4545 Trearddur Road. The Leisure Centre and field is on the right ½ mile from the roundabout.

HOLYWELL TOWN FC

Founded: Circa 1880 (as Holywell FC)
Former Names: Holywell FC, Holywell Victoria FC, Holywell Arcadians FC and Holywell United FC
Nickname: 'The Wellmen'
Ground: Halkyn Road Ground, Halkyn Street, Holywell, Flintshire CH5 7NE
Ground Telephone Nº: None

Club Colours: Red & White striped shirts, Red shorts
Correspondence: Mr I. Laidlaw-Wilson, 5 Pistyll, Holywell, Flintshire CH8 7SH
Contact Telephone Nº: (01352) 711538
Fax Number: None
E-mail: r101vcc@aol.com

GENERAL INFORMATION
Club Shop: None
Car Parking: At the ground
Coach Parking: At the ground
Nearest Railway Station: Flint (4 miles)
Nearest Bus Station: Holywell (½ mile)
Nearest Police Station: Holywell
Police Telephone Nº: (01352) 711669

GROUND INFORMATION
Ground Capacity: 3,000
Seating Capacity: 300
Record Attendance: Approximately 3,000
Pitch Size: 115 x 72 yards

ADMISSION INFO (2003/2004 PRICES)
Adult Standing: £3.00
Adult Seating: £3.00
Child Standing: £1.50
Child Seating: £1.50
Programme Price: £1.00

DISABLED SUPPORTERS INFORMATION
Wheelchairs: Accommodated
Disabled Toilets: Available
Contact Number: (01352) 711538

Travelling Supporters' Information:
Routes: From the Town Centre: Proceed down Halkyn Road past the Police Station and the ground is situated on the left down an approach road (clearly signposted) at the rear of the Health Centre; From South Wales, Merseyside and the South: Follow the A55 Expressway and follow signs for Conwy until you reach the Holywell sliproad, A5026. The ground is on the right after 1 mile.

LEX XI FC

Founded: 1965
Former Names: None
Nickname: None
Ground: Stansty Park, Mold Road, Summerhill, Wrexham, North Wales
Ground Telephone Nº: None

Club Colours: Amber shirts and shorts
Correspondence: Steve Lloyd, Elm Cottage, Middle Sontley, Wrexham   LL13 0YP
Contact Telephone Nº: (01978) 844430
Fax Number: None

GENERAL INFORMATION

Social Club Telephone Nº: (01978) 261351
Club Shop: None
Car Parking: At the ground
Coach Parking: At the ground
Nearest Railway Station: Wrexham (2 miles)
Nearest Bus Station: King Street, Wrexham (1 mile)
Nearest Police Station: Wrexham
Police Telephone Nº: (01978) 290222

GROUND INFORMATION

Ground Capacity: 2,000
Seating Capacity: 50
Record Attendance: 1,004 vs Wrexham (1989)
Pitch Size: 108 x 74 yards

ADMISSION INFO (2003/2004 PRICES)

Adult Standing: £2.00
Adult Seating: £2.00
Child Standing: £1.00
Child Seating: £1.00
Concessionary Standing: £1.00
Concessionary Seating: £1.00
Programme Price: 50p

DISABLED SUPPORTERS INFORMATION

Wheelchairs: Accommodated
Disabled Toilets: None
Contact Number: (01978) 844430

Travelling Supporters' Information:
Routes: The ground is situated on a triangular piece of land known as Stansty Park in between Summerhill Road and Mold Road on the outskirts of Wrexham, 2 miles from the Town Centre and 1 mile from Wrexham FC's Racecourse Ground.

LLANDUDNO FC

Founded: 1988
Former Names: Llandudno Town FC
Nickname: None
Ground: Maesdu Park, Builder Street West, Llandudno, Conwy
Ground Telephone Nº: (01492) 860945

Club Colours: Sky Blue and Navy Blue shirts with Navy Blue shorts
Correspondence Address: Dorothy Montgomery, 9 Fford Gwynedd, Llandudno, Conwy
Contact Telephone Nº: (01492) 876574
Web Site: www.llandudnofc.co.uk
E-mail: doz@montol.fsnet.co.uk

GENERAL INFORMATION
Club Shop: Yes – in the Clubhouse
Car Parking: At the ground
Coach Parking: At the ground
Nearest Railway Station: Llandudno (½ mile)
Nearest Bus Station: Llandudno Junction
Nearest Police Station: Llandudno
Police Telephone Nº: (01492) 860260

GROUND INFORMATION
Ground Capacity: 6,000
Seating Capacity: 130
Record Attendance: 1,600 vs Everton
Pitch Size: 110 x 70 yards

ADMISSION INFO (2003/2004 PRICES)
Adult Standing: £3.00
Adult Seating: £3.00
Child Standing: £1.00 (free when with an adult)
Child Seating: £1.00 (free when with an adult)
Concessionary Standing: £2.00
Concessionary Seating: £2.00
Programme Price: 50p

DISABLED SUPPORTERS INFORMATION
Wheelchairs: Accommodated
Disabled Toilets: None
Contact Number: (01492) 860945

Travelling Supporters' Information:
Routes: Take the A55 Expressway to the Llandudno Junction exit (next to the Conwy Tunnel) and take the 2nd exit at the roundabout for Deganwy (A546). Pass through Deganwy and head into Llandudno. After the Golf Course take a right hand turn before the railway bridge then 1st left into Builder Street West. The ground is on the right next to the coach park; Alternative Route: Take the A55 Expressway to the Betws-y-Coed/Llandudno turn-off. Follow signs for Llandudno (A470) and then follow the road to the Links Hotel roundabout. Turn left past the Rugby field and take the next right. The ground is on the right next to the coach park.

LLANFAIRPWLL FC

Founded: 1898 (Re-formed 1972)
Former Names: None
Ground: Gors Field, Llanfairpwll, Anglesey
Ground Telephone Nº: None
Colours: Blue and Navy shirts with White shorts

Correspondence: A. Mummery, 39 Trem Eryri,
Llanfairpwll, Anglesey
Contact Tel. Nº: (01248) 714938
Fax Number: None
Web Site: www.31cilygraig.freeserve.co.uk/Peldroed

GENERAL INFORMATION
Club Shop: At the ground – Matchdays only
Car Parking: At the ground
Coach Parking: At the ground
Nearest Railway Station: Llanfairpwll
Nearest Bus Station: Llanfairpwll
Nearest Police Station: Menai Bridge
Police Telephone Nº: –

GROUND INFORMATION
Ground Capacity: 750
Seating Capacity: 50
Record Attendance: 523 (during 2001)
Pitch Size: 110 x 70 yards

ADMISSION INFO (2003/2004 PRICES)
Adult Standing: £2.00
Adult Seating: £2.00
Child Standing: £1.00
Child Seating: £1.00
Programme Price: 50p

DISABLED SUPPORTERS INFORMATION
Wheelchairs: Accommodated
Disabled Toilets: Yes
Contact Number: (01248) 714938

Travelling Supporters' Information:
Routes: Take the A55 over the Menai Bridge and once across turn left towards Llanfairpwll. Pass the monument on the right, turn off for Plas Newydd on the left and head towards the Railway Station Centre. Just before the Railway Station Shopping Centre turn right into the car park for the ground.

LLANGEFNI TOWN FC

Founded: 1897
Former Names: Llangefni FC, Llangefni/Glantraeth FC
Nickname: 'The Dazzlers'
Ground: Cae Bob Parry, Talwrn Road, Llangefni, Anglesey
Ground Telephone Nº: (01248) 724999

Club Colours: Yellow shirts and shorts
Correspondence Address: Terry Roberts, 13 Bryn Tawel, Bryn Siencyn, Llanfairpwll, LL61 6RJ
Contact Tel. Nº: (07944) 717699
Fax Number: (01248) 724165

GENERAL INFORMATION

Club Shop: None
Car Parking: At the ground
Coach Parking: At the ground
Nearest Railway Station: Llanfair PG
Nearest Bus Station: Llangefni
Nearest Police Station: Llangefni
Police Telephone Nº: (01248) 722222

GROUND INFORMATION

Ground Capacity: 1,500
Seating Capacity: 200
Record Attendance: 250
Pitch Size: 110 x 75 yards

ADMISSION INFO (2003/2004 PRICES)

Adult Standing: £3.00
Adult Seating: £3.00
Child Standing: £2.00
Child Seating: £2.00
Programme Price: £1.00

DISABLED SUPPORTERS INFORMATION

Wheelchairs: Accommodated
Disabled Toilets: Available
Contact Number: (07944) 717699

Travelling Supporters' Information:
Routes: Take the A55 Expressway to Anglesey and exit at the Llangefni turnoff following the A5114 towards Llangefni. Before entering town, turn right at the Industrial Estate sign. Take the 1st exit at the roundabout and follow the road to the T-junction. Turn right and go past Kwik Save on the left. Follow the road up the hill past K.J. Forge Garage on the right and then turn left at the junction by the phone box into Talwrn Road (marked Pentraeth B5109). Continue for about ½ mile then turn left for the ground.

MOLD ALEXANDRA FC

Founded: 1929
Former Names: None
Nickname: 'The Alex'
Ground: Alyn Park, Mold, Flintshire
Ground Telephone Nº: (01352) 750816

Colours: Blue shirts and shorts
Correspondence: G. Hampson, 4 Llys Mervyn, Denbigh Road, Mold   CH7 1XR
Contact Telephone Nº: (01352) 758675
Fax Number: (01244) 677769
Web Site: www.moldalexfc.com
E-mail: gazhampson@btinternet.com

GENERAL INFORMATION
Club Shop: Available via the Secretary
Car Parking: At the ground
Coach Parking: At the ground
Nearest Railway Station: Buckley (3 miles)
Nearest Bus Station: Mold
Nearest Police Station: Mold
Police Telephone Nº: (01352) 752321

GROUND INFORMATION
Ground Capacity: 2,000
Seating Capacity: 105
Record Attendance: Not known
Pitch Size: 112 x 75 yards

ADMISSION INFO (2003/2004 PRICES)
Adult Standing: £3.00
Adult Seating: £3.00
Child Standing: Free of charge
Child Seating: Free of charge
Programme Price: 50p

DISABLED SUPPORTERS INFORMATION
Wheelchairs: Accommodated
Disabled Toilets: None
Contact Number: (01352) 758675

Travelling Supporters' Information:
Routes: The ground is situated on Denbigh Road. From Mold town centre follow signs for Denbigh. The approach road is on the right hand side of Denbigh Road, 100 yards before the Blue Bell Pub.

RUTHIN TOWN FC

Founded: 1951
Former Names: Ruthin British Legion FC
Nickname: 'Town'
Ground: Memorial Playing Fields, Parc-y-Dre, Ruthin, Denbighshire
Ground Telephone Nº: None

Colours: Blue shirts and shorts
Correspondence: Bryn Evans, Dyffryn, Llanrhaedr, Denbigh   LL16 4NT
Contact Telephone Nº: (07789) 022133
Fax Number: None

GENERAL INFORMATION
Club Shop: None
Car Parking: At the ground
Coach Parking: At the ground
Nearest Railway Station: Rhyl
Nearest Bus Station: Rhyl – then Services 151/152
Nearest Police Station: Ruthin (1 mile)
Police Telephone Nº: (01824) 702041

GROUND INFORMATION
Ground Capacity: 2,000
Seating Capacity: 50
Record Attendance: 2,000
Pitch Size: 115 x 75 yards

ADMISSION INFO (2003/2004 PRICES)
Adult Standing: £3.00
Adult Seating: £3.00
Child Standing: 50p
Child Seating: 50p
Concessionary Standing: £1.00
Concessionary Seating: £1.00
Programme Price: 75p

DISABLED SUPPORTERS INFORMATION
Wheelchairs: Accommodated
Disabled Toilets: None
Contact Number: (07789) 022133

Travelling Supporters' Information:
Routes: The ground is situated on Park Road (A494). Turn into Parc-y-Dre next to the Fire Station and take the first right turn for the ground.

Welsh Premier League 2002/2003	Aberystwyth Town	Afan Lido	Bangor City	Barry Town	Caernarfon Town	Caersws	Carmarthen Town	Connah's Quay Nomads	Cwmbran Town	Flexsys Cefn Druids	Haverfordwest County	Llanelli	Newtown	Oswestry Town	Port Talbot Town	Rhyl	Total Network Solutions	Welshpool Town
Aberystwyth Town		0-0	0-1	3-1	1-1	1-3	2-0	3-1	1-1	3-0	2-1	2-0	3-1	5-1	1-0	1-1	2-2	0-0
Afan Lido	1-1		1-2	0-1	0-1	1-0	2-0	3-0	1-2	0-3	0-0	2-2	1-2	0-0	2-0	1-1	0-6	2-0
Bangor City	0-1	2-1		1-1	3-1	5-0	3-2	2-1	2-1	2-0	2-1	8-0	0-1	2-2	3-0	1-0	0-2	3-1
Barry Town	5-1	1-0	3-0		3-2	3-2	3-0	3-1	2-1	6-0	3-0	1-0	2-2	4-0	0-1	4-1	0-0	2-1
Caernarfon Town	0-3	1-1	2-2	1-4		1-2	2-1	2-0	3-1	3-3	0-1	1-1	1-2	1-1	2-1	0-2	1-1	0-0
Caersws	2-2	1-2	1-1	0-1	2-1		4-1	1-0	1-1	2-1	1-1	4-0	1-0	2-3	3-1	2-2	0-4	3-1
Carmarthen Town	0-2	0-2	0-6	2-2	0-3	3-1		1-1	0-4	0-1	0-2	2-1	1-4	2-1	0-2	0-3	1-1	5-1
Connah's Quay N.	2-1	2-1	2-1	0-2	1-1	1-3	1-0		1-1	4-1	3-1	3-0	1-0	2-4	2-2	2-1	0-1	4-0
Cwmbran Town	2-1	0-2	0-0	2-3	1-0	3-2	4-0	0-2		0-0	3-1	3-2	2-1	0-0	1-1	2-0	0-0	4-0
Flexsys Cefn Druids	3-0	0-1	0-2	0-3	2-1	0-1	0-1	0-0	1-0		0-1	4-0	3-0	0-0	3-2	0-2	0-1	0-2
Haverfordwest Co.	0-3	1-4	0-4	2-4	3-1	3-2	0-2	1-3	4-0	2-4		2-3	2-2	0-2	2-1	1-5	0-3	0-0
Llanelli	2-3	1-3	2-5	2-3	3-3	3-2	1-2	3-5	0-3	3-1	1-3		2-3	3-1	0-2	0-3	2-3	0-1
Newtown	3-1	1-2	2-1	0-0	0-3	0-2	2-2	1-2	4-1	1-2	4-0	2-1		1-3	2-4	0-2	2-4	0-2
Oswestry Town	0-1	0-3	1-2	0-4	3-0	0-2	1-2	2-3	0-5	0-1	1-1	3-1	0-0		0-0	2-3	0-3	1-1
Port Talbot Town	0-1	0-2	0-2	0-5	3-2	0-0	0-2	0-1	1-0	2-1	3-0	1-1	0-2	4-1		0-3	1-1	1-0
Rhyl	0-0	2-2	0-1	0-1	1-0	4-0	1-0	1-2	2-1	1-0	1-0	1-1	1-2	1-1	3-0		0-1	2-0
Total Net. Solutions	3-0	1-1	4-2	1-0	0-2	2-1	2-0	2-0	1-0	2-0	1-2	3-1	1-1	2-1	1-0	5-0		2-0
Welshpool Town	1-3	0-0	1-4	0-4	1-0	0-4	1-1	1-2	1-2	3-3	0-2	1-0	1-0	6-1	2-3	0-2	1-2	

JT Hughes Mitsubishi Welsh Premier League

Season 2002/2003

Team	P	W	D	L	F	A	Pts
Barry Town	34	26	5	3	84	26	83
Total Network Solutions	34	24	8	2	68	21	80
Bangor City	34	22	5	7	75	34	71
Aberystwyth Town	34	17	9	8	54	38	60
Connah's Quay Nomads	34	18	5	11	55	46	59
Rhyl	34	17	7	10	52	33	58
Afan Lido	34	14	10	10	44	34	52
Caersws	34	15	6	13	57	52	51
Cwmbran Town	34	14	8	12	51	40	50
Newtown	34	12	6	16	48	54	42
Port Talbot Town	34	11	6	17	36	51	39
Flexsys Cefn Druids	34	11	5	18	37	51	38
Haverfordwest County	34	10	5	19	40	68	35
Caernarfon Town	34	8	10	16	43	53	34
Carmarthen Town	34	9	5	20	33	66	32
Oswestry Town	34	6	10	18	36	67	28
Welshpool Town	34	7	7	20	30	62	28
Llanelli	34	4	5	25	42	89	17

Champions: Barry Town

Relegated: Llanelli, Welshpool Town and Oswestry Town

HGF Cymru Alliance

Season 2002/2003

Porthmadog	32	28	2	2	106	19	86
Llandudno	32	20	7	5	81	41	67
Buckley Town	32	19	7	6	86	34	64
Llangefni Town	32	21	1	10	78	39	64
Airbus UK	32	17	5	10	70	50	56
Ruthin Town	32	17	3	12	79	45	54
Halkyn United	32	14	9	9	56	57	51
Amlwch Town	32	11	9	12	45	55	42
Lex XI	32	13	5	14	83	72	41
Holyhead Hotspurs	32	11	8	13	60	62	41
Flint Town United	32	11	7	14	50	61	40
Mold Alexandra	32	8	7	17	35	56	31
Gresford Athletic	32	8	6	18	52	64	30
Llanfairpwll	32	8	5	19	35	66	29
Guilsfield	32	7	7	18	43	86	28
Cemaes Bay	32	7	3	22	41	130	24
Holywell Town	32	4	5	23	33	96	8

Promoted: Porthmadog

Welsh Football League Division Two

Season 2002/2003

Dinas Powys	34	24	7	3	97	31	79
Grange Harlequins	34	22	6	6	95	46	72
Bridgend Town	34	21	9	4	73	33	72
AFC Llwydcoed	34	18	11	5	67	33	65
Taffs Well	34	15	7	12	65	54	52
Newport YMCA	34	15	7	12	50	46	52
Pontypridd Town	34	12	15	7	62	41	51
Aberaman Athletic	34	14	8	12	69	65	50
Tredegar Town	34	14	6	14	70	63	48
Ammanford	34	14	5	15	65	63	47
Blaenrhondda	34	13	4	17	45	70	43
Treharris Athletic	34	10	10	14	55	55	40
Morriston Town	34	11	6	17	55	76	39
Merthyr Saints	34	11	5	18	50	69	38
Porthcawl Town	34	10	4	20	55	98	34
Porth Tywyn Suburbs	34	9	5	20	52	79	32
AFC Rhondda	34	8	7	19	48	73	31
Fields Park Pontllanfraith	34	3	2	29	36	114	11

Promoted: Dinas Powys, Grange Harlequins and Bridgend Town

Relegated: Fields Park Pontllanfraith, AFC Rhondda and Porth Tywyn Suburbs

Welsh Football League Division One

Season 2002/2003

Bettws	34	24	5	5	89	30	77
Neath AFC	34	24	5	5	70	29	77
UWIC Inter Cardiff	34	23	7	4	67	33	76
Ton Pentre	34	22	3	9	86	34	69
Goytre United	34	19	3	12	56	39	60
Garw	34	15	6	13	60	57	51
Briton Ferry Athletic	34	14	5	15	50	53	47
Cardiff Civil Service	34	12	9	13	45	52	45
Maesteg Park	34	13	6	15	44	57	45
Pontardawe	34	12	7	15	51	49	43
Cardiff Corinthians	34	12	6	16	40	58	42
Caerleon	34	10	10	14	48	48	40
Llanwern	34	11	5	18	44	64	38
Gwynfi United	34	10	7	17	56	57	37
Ely Rangers	34	10	6	18	46	51	36
Garden Village	34	9	7	18	39	65	34
Penrhiwceiber Rangers	34	9	7	18	47	80	34
Milford United	34	1	8	25	26	108	11

Champions: Bettws

Relegated: Milford United, Penrhiwceiber Rangers and Garden Village

Welsh Football League Division Three

Season 2002/2003

Pontyclun	34	21	7	6	73	39	70
Skewen Athletic	34	22	4	8	78	45	70
Caldicot Town	34	19	8	7	69	43	65
Caerau Ely	34	19	7	8	77	46	64
Bryntirion Athletic	34	19	4	11	70	41	61
Seven Sisters	34	15	7	12	59	53	52
Troedyrhiw	34	15	5	14	53	52	50
Pontlottyn Blast Furnace	34	14	8	12	70	72	50
Treowen Stars	34	13	7	14	50	48	46
Tillery	34	11	10	13	64	72	43
Albion Rovers	34	11	7	16	54	64	40
Risca & Gelli United	34	10	9	15	53	65	39
Cwmamman Town	34	11	5	18	57	70	38
Chepstow Town	34	10	8	16	67	84	38
Pentwyn Dynamos	34	9	8	17	59	70	35
Newcastle Emlyn	34	10	5	19	51	75	35
RTB Ebbw Vale	34	10	3	21	52	82	33
Caerau	34	8	6	20	58	93	30

Promoted: Pontyclun, Skewen Athletic and Caldicot Town

THE WELSH FOOTBALL LEAGUE

Address
Ken Tucker, 16 The Parade,
Merthyr Tydfil   CF47 0ET

Phone (01685) 723844   **Fax** (01685) 723844

Division One Clubs for the 2003/2004 Season

Bettws FC .... Page 50

Bridgend Town FC .... Page 51

Briton Ferry Athletic FC .... Page 52

Caerleon FC .... Page 53

Cardiff Corinthians FC .... Page 54

Dinas Powys FC .... Page 55

Ely Rangers FC .... Page 56

Garw FC .... Page 57

Goytre United FC .... Page 58

Grange Harlequins FC .... Page 59

Gwynfi United FC .... Page 60

Llanelli FC .... Page 61

Llanwern FC .... Page 62

Maesteg Park FC .... Page 63

Neath FC .... Page 64

Pontardawe Town FC .... Page 65

Ton Pentre FC .... Page 66

UWIC Inter Cardiff FC .... Page 67

BETTWS FC

Founded: 1995
Former Names: Formed by the amalgamation of
Bettws Athletic FC and Bettws AFC
Nickname: None
Ground: Bettws Park, North Site, Bettws,
near Bridgend, Mid Glamorgan
Ground Phone Nº: (01656) 725618 (Clubhouse)

Colours: Blue & White quartered shirts, White shorts
Correspondence: Phil Sweeney, 44 Hazelmead,
Bryn Menyn, Bridgend CF32 9AQ
Contact Telephone Nº: (01656) 724978/729682
Fax Number: (01656) 724978

GENERAL INFORMATION
Clubhouse Phone Nº: (01656) 725618 (Oddfellows Arms)
Club Shop: At the Oddfellows Arms
Car Parking: At the ground
Coach Parking: At the ground
Nearest Railway Station: Bridgend (4 miles)
Nearest Bus Station: Bridgend
Nearest Police Station: Aberken Fig
Police Telephone Nº: –

GROUND INFORMATION
Ground Capacity: 1,000
Seating Capacity: None
Record Attendance: Approximately 800 (2001)
Pitch Size: 110 x 72 yards

ADMISSION INFO (2003/2004 PRICES)
Adult Standing: £2.00
Child Standing: £1.00
Concessionary Standing: £1.00
Programme Price: Included with admission

DISABLED SUPPORTERS INFORMATION
Wheelchairs: Accommodated in the Stand
Disabled Toilets: None
Contact Number: (01656) 725618

Travelling Supporters' Information:
Routes: Exit the M4 at Junction 36 and follow signs for Maesteg on the A4063. Go past the entrance to Sarn Park Services and at the roundabout take the 3rd exit signposted Maesteg (A4063). Continue until the traffic lights and turn right (signposted Bryn Cethin) onto the A4065. After ¾ mile pass under 2 railway bridges and pass the green on the right. Go straight on for 500 yards, turn left at the Bettws sign and follow the road into the village for 1½ miles. Pass the Oddfellows Arms and continue up the hill – the ground is situated on the left at the edge of the village.

BRIDGEND TOWN FC

Founded: 1954
Former Names: Bridgend Vics FC
Nickname: None
Ground: Coychurch Road, Bridgend, Mid Glamorgan
Ground Tel. Nº: (01656) 655097

Colours: Sky Blue & White shirts, Navy Blue shorts
Correspondence: Colin Mawer, Pine Lodge, Derwen, Bridgend   CF35 6HD
Contact Tel. Nº: (01656) 650444
Fax Number: None

GENERAL INFORMATION

Club Shop: None
Car Parking: At the ground
Coach Parking: At the ground
Nearest Railway Station: Bridgend (¼ mile)
Nearest Bus Station: Bridgend
Nearest Police Station: Bridgend
Police Telephone Nº: (01656) 655555

GROUND INFORMATION

Ground Capacity: 5,000
Seating Capacity: 200
Record Attendance: Approximately 5,000
Pitch Size: 104 x 71 yards

ADMISSION INFO (2002/2003 PRICES)

Adult Standing: £2.00 (by programme)
Adult Seating: £2.00 (by programme)
Child Standing: £1.00 (by programme)
Child Seating: £1.00 (by programme)
Concessionary Standing: £1.00 (by programme)
Concessionary Seating: £1.00 (by programme)
Programme Price: Included in admission price

DISABLED SUPPORTERS INFORMATION

Wheelchairs: Accommodated
Disabled Toilets: None
Contact Number: (01656) 650444

Travelling Supporters' Information:
Routes: Exit the M4 at Junction 35 and bear left at the first roundabout. At the 2nd roundabout take the 3rd exit. Go past Tesco and Bridgend College on the left then turn right at the Fish & Chip shop into Coychurch Road. The ground entrance is approximately 100 yards on the right.

BRITON FERRY ATHLETIC FC

Founded: 1926/27
Former Names: None
Nickname: None
Ground: Old Road, Briton Ferry, Neath, West Glamorgan
Ground Telephone Nº: (01639) 812458

Club Colours: Red shirts and shorts
Correspondence: Gary Hughes, 17 Morgans Terrace, Cwrt Sart, Briton Ferry, SA11 2SY
Contact Telephone Nº: (01639) 790656
Fax Number: (01639) 812458

GENERAL INFORMATION
Club Shop: None
Car Parking: Street parking
Coach Parking: By Police direction
Nearest Railway Station: Neath (3 miles)
Nearest Bus Station: Neath (3 miles)
Nearest Police Station: Briton Ferry
Police Telephone Nº: (01639) 812220

GROUND INFORMATION
Ground Capacity: 2,000
Seating Capacity: 300
Record Attendance: 800 vs Abergavenny (1991/92)
Pitch Size: 112 x 75 yards

ADMISSION INFO (2003/2004 PRICES)
Adult Standing: £2.00 (by programme)
Adult Seating: £2.00 (by programme)
Child Standing: £1.00 (by programme)
Child Seating: £1.00 (by programme)
Programme Price: Included in admission

DISABLED SUPPORTERS INFORMATION
Wheelchairs: Accommodated
Disabled Toilets: None
Contact Number: (01639) 812458

Travelling Supporters' Information:
Routes: Take the M4 then the A48 and turn right at the roundabout for Briton Ferry then right again at the traffic lights and the ground is situated on the right; From Neath Railway Station: Turn right along Main Street, go under the subway at the junction, turn right into Briton Ferry Road, left into Cryddan Road and continue for 1½ miles past the Hospital. The ground is on the left.

CAERLEON FC

Founded: 1889
Former Names: None
Nickname: None
Ground: Cold Bath Road, Caerleon, Gwent
Ground Telephone Nº: (01633) 420074

Club Colours: Green and White shirts and shorts
Correspondence Address: P.J. Roden, Hen Gartref, Caerleon Road, Ponthir, Newport   NP18 1PG
Contact Telephone Nº: (01633) 420074
Fax Number: (01633) 420074

GENERAL INFORMATION
Social Club Telephone Nº: (01633) 420074
Club Shop: None
Car Parking: At the ground
Coach Parking: At the ground
Nearest Railway Station: Newport (4 miles)
Nearest Bus Station: Newport
Nearest Police Station: Caerleon
Police Telephone Nº: (01633) 420222

GROUND INFORMATION
Ground Capacity: 1,200
Seating Capacity: None
Record Attendance: 1,000
Pitch Size: 117 x 74 yards

ADMISSION INFO (2003/2004 PRICES)
Adult Standing: £2.00 (by programme)
Child Standing: £2.00 (by programme)
Programme Price: £2.00 (includes admission)

DISABLED SUPPORTERS INFORMATION
Wheelchairs: Accommodated
Disabled Toilets: None
Contact Number: (01633) 420074

Travelling Supporters' Information:
Routes: From the East: Exit the M4 at Junction 25 and follow signs to Caerleon. In Caerleon at the junction of Lodge Road, turn left into Cold Bath Road for the ground. From the West: Exit the M4 at Junction 25 and follow signs to Caerleon. Then as above.

CARDIFF CORINTHIANS FC

Founded: 1898
Former Names: None
Nickname: 'Corries'
Ground: Riverside Ground, Thro' Stadium Road, Radyr, near Cardiff
Ground Telephone Nº: (029) 2084-3407

Club Colours: Cardinal & Gold shirts, Cardinal shorts
Correspondence Address: Glynn Dudley, 17 Bridgwater Road, Llanrumney, Cardiff CF3 9TF
Contact Telephone Nº: (029) 2021-8871
Fax Number: None

GENERAL INFORMATION

Club Shop: None
Car Parking: At the ground
Coach Parking: At the ground
Nearest Railway Station: Radyr (adjacent)
Nearest Bus Station: Cardiff
Nearest Police Station: Cowbridge Road, Canton
Police Telephone Nº: (029) 2022-2111

GROUND INFORMATION

Ground Capacity: 1,000
Seating Capacity: None
Record Attendance: Not known
Pitch Size: 110 x 75 yards

ADMISSION INFO (2003/2004 PRICES)

Adult Standing: £2.00 (by programme)
Child Standing: Free of charge
Programme Price: Included with admission

DISABLED SUPPORTERS INFORMATION

Wheelchairs: Accommodated
Disabled Toilets: None
Contact Number: (029) 2084-3407

Travelling Supporters' Information:
Routes: Exit the M4 at Junction 32 and take the A470 signposted for Merthyr. After 1½ miles take the B4262 for Radyr. On entering the village (after approximately 2½ miles), turn left by the shops and go towards the Railway Station. Pass under the railway bridge, turn right and the ground is at the Radyr Cricket Club adjacent.

DINAS POWYS FC

Founded: 1974
Former Names: Swan Stars FC
Nickname: None
Ground: Murchfield, Sunnycroft Lane, Dinas Powys
Ground Tel. Nº: None

Club Colours: White shirts with Red shorts
Correspondence: Jerry McIntyre, 19 Croffta,
Dinas Powys CF64 4UN
Contact Tel. Nº: (029) 2051-4913
Fax Number: None

GENERAL INFORMATION
Club Shop: None
Car Parking: 30 spaces available at the ground
Coach Parking: None
Nearest Railway Station: Dinas Powys (¼ mile)
Nearest Bus Station: Cardiff Central (3½ miles)
Nearest Police Station: Barry
Police Telephone Nº: (01446) 734451

GROUND INFORMATION
Ground Capacity: 1,000
Seating Capacity: None
Record Attendance: Approximately 450 vs Barry Town
Pitch Size: 105 x 70 yards

ADMISSION INFO (2003/2004 PRICES)
Adult Standing: £2.50
Child Seating: Free of charge
Programme Price: £1.00

DISABLED SUPPORTERS INFORMATION
Wheelchairs: Accommodated
Disabled Toilets: Available
Contact Number: (029) 2051-4913

Travelling Supporters' Information:
Routes: Exit the M4 at Junction 33 onto the A4232 (3rd exit signposted Leckwith). Follow signs for Dinas Powys, turn left at the traffic lights by Dinas Powys Infants School, 2nd right into Camms Corner then 2nd right into Sunnycroft Lane. The ground is situated at the bottom of the road.

ELY RANGERS FC

Founded: 1965
Former Names: None
Nickname: 'The Griffins'
Ground: Station Road, Wenvoe, Cardiff
Ground Telephone Nº: (029) 2059-8725

Colours: Black and Blue striped shirts, Black shorts
Correspondence: Bob Fry, 4 Fairmead Court, Fairwater, Cardiff   CF5 3DD
Contact Telephone Nº: (029) 2056-6762

GENERAL INFORMATION

Club Shop: None
Car Parking: At the ground
Coach Parking: At the ground
Nearest Railway Station: Cardiff Central   (6 miles)
Nearest Bus Station: Cardiff
Nearest Police Station: Fairwater
Police Telephone Nº: (029) 2022-2111

GROUND INFORMATION

Ground Capacity: 1,000
Seating Capacity: None
Record Attendance: Approximately 1,000
Pitch Size: 110 x 75 yards

ADMISSION INFO (2003/2004 PRICES)

Adult Standing: £2.00
Child Standing: £1.00
Concessionary Standing: £1.00
Programme Price: 50p

DISABLED SUPPORTERS INFORMATION

Wheelchairs: Accommodated
Disabled Toilets: None
Contact Number: (029) 2056-6762

Travelling Supporters' Information:
Routes: Exit the M4 at Junction 33 and take the A4232 following signs for Cardiff Wales Airport. At Culverhouse Cross roundabout take the 3rd exit onto the A4050 Barry/Cardiff Wales Airport road. Go straight on at three mini-roundabouts and turn left in front of the grey footbridge over the road. This road is Station Road Wenvoe and the ground is 400 yards on the right.

GARW FC

Founded: 1945
Former Names: Garw Athletic FC
Nickname: 'Athletic'
Ground: Blandy Park, Pontycymer, near Bridgend, South Wales
Ground Telephone Nº: None

Colours: Red shirts and shorts
Correspondence: Ray Smiles, 48 Blaengarw Road, Blaengarw, Mid Glamorgan
Contact Telephone Nº: (01656) 870487
Fax Number: None

GENERAL INFORMATION

Club Shop: None
Car Parking: Street parking only
Coach Parking: Street parking only
Nearest Railway Station: Tondu (4 miles)
Nearest Bus Station: Bridgend (10 miles)
Nearest Police Station: Aberkenfig
Police Telephone Nº: –

GROUND INFORMATION

Ground Capacity: 1,000
Seating Capacity: None
Record Attendance: Not known
Pitch Size: 110 x 65 yards

ADMISSION INFO (2003/2004 PRICES)

Adult Standing: £2.00 (by programme)
Child Standing: Free of charge
Programme Price: £2.00 (included in admission)

DISABLED SUPPORTERS INFORMATION

Wheelchairs: Accommodated
Disabled Toilets: None
Contact Number: (01656) 871906

Travelling Supporters' Information:
Routes: Exit the M4 at Junction 36 and take the A4061 to Bryncethin. Turn left onto the A4064 and continue to Pontycymer. Upon reaching Pontycymer take the first left after the town sign for the ground.

GOYTRE UNITED FC

Founded: 1963
Former Names: None
Nickname: 'Goyts'
Ground: Glenhafod Park, Goytre, Port Talbot, West Glamorgan
Ground Telephone Nº: (01639) 898983

Colours: Blue and White shirts with Blue shorts
Correspondence: Lyndon Suhanski, Stoneydale, Parc Pen y Bryn, Goytre, Port Talbot SA13 2XZ
Contact Telephone Nº: (01639) 894805
Fax Number: (01639) 898983
Web Site: www.goytreunitedafc.com
E-mail: goytreunitedafc@hotmail.com

GENERAL INFORMATION
Club Shop: None
Car Parking: At the ground
Coach Parking: At the ground
Nearest Railway Station: Port Talbot General (1½ miles)
Nearest Bus Station: Port Talbot General (2 miles)
Nearest Police Station: Port Talbot
Police Telephone Nº: (01639) 883101

GROUND INFORMATION
Ground Capacity: 4,000
Seating Capacity: 280
Record Attendance: Not known
Pitch Size: 110 x 70 yards

ADMISSION INFO (2003/2004 PRICES)
Adult Standing: £2.00
Adult Seating: £2.00
Child Standing: 50p
Child Seating: 50p
Concessionary Standing: £1.00
Concessionary Seating: £1.00
Programme Price: 50p

DISABLED SUPPORTERS INFORMATION
Wheelchairs: Accommodated
Disabled Toilets: None
Contact Number: (01639) 898983

Travelling Supporters' Information:
Routes: Exit the M4 at Junction 40, bear left at the mini-roundabout and follow signs for Goytre. Turn left at the T-junction and the ground is ½ mile on the left.

GRANGE HARLEQUINS FC

Founded: 1935
Former Names: Grange Juniors FC
Nickname: 'The Quins'
Ground: Cardiff Athletic Stadium, Leckwith, Cardiff
Ground Tel. Nº: (029) 2022-5345

Colours: Red & White quartered shirts, White shorts
Correspondence: Malcolm Stammers,
90 Beulah Road, Rhiwbina, Cardiff   CF14 6LZ
Contact Tel. Nº: (029) 2061-1532
Fax Number: None

GENERAL INFORMATION
Car Parking: 1,600 space car park next to the ground
Coach Parking: Space for 30 coaches next to the ground
Nearest Railway Station: Grangetown
Nearest Bus Station: Cardiff Central
Nearest Police Station: Canton
Police Telephone Nº: (029) 2022-2111

GROUND INFORMATION
Ground Capacity: 5,000
Seating Capacity: 2,500
Record Attendance: 1,219 vs Cwmbran Town (Welsh Cup)
Pitch Size: 110 x 76 yards

ADMISSION INFO (2003/2004 PRICES)
Adult Standing: £2.00
Adult Seating: £2.00
Child Standing: £1.00
Child Seating: £1.00
Programme Price: Included with admission

DISABLED SUPPORTERS INFORMATION
Wheelchairs: Accommodated – Lift access in Grandstand
Disabled Toilets: Available
Contact Number: (029) 2022-5345

Travelling Supporters' Information:
Routes: Exit the M4 at Junction 33 and take the 3rd exit (Leckwith Interchange) signposted for "Athletics Stadium and Leckwith Industrial Estate". Take the 1st exit at the next roundabout onto the B4267 (Leckwith Road). The Stadium us situated on the right after 200 yards.

GWYNFI UNITED FC

Founded: 1971
Former Names: Gwynfi Welfare FC
Nickname: None
Ground: Gwynfi Welfare, Blaengwynfi, Port Talbot, West Glamorgan
Ground Telephone Nº: (01639) 898983

Club Colours: Green shirts with Black shorts
Correspondence: David Walters, 144 Jersey Road, Blaengwynfi, Port Talbot   SA13 3TF
Contact Telephone Nº: (01639) 851506
Fax Number: (01656) 812145

GENERAL INFORMATION
Social Club Telephone Nº: None
Club Shop: None
Car Parking: At the ground
Coach Parking: At the ground
Nearest Railway Station: Port Talbot (10 miles)
Nearest Bus Station: Port Talbot (10 miles)
Nearest Police Station: Cymmer
Police Telephone Nº: (01639) 883101

GROUND INFORMATION
Ground Capacity: 1,500
Seating Capacity: None
Record Attendance: Not known
Pitch Size: 110 x 71 yards

ADMISSION INFO (2003/2004 PRICES)
Adult Standing: £2.00 (by programme)
Child Standing: Free of charge
Programme Price: £2.00 (includes admission)

DISABLED SUPPORTERS INFORMATION
Wheelchairs: Accommodated
Disabled Toilets: None
Contact Number: (01639) 898983

Travelling Supporters' Information:
Routes: Exit the M4 at Junction 36 and follow the A4063 to Maesteg. Pass through Maesteg and take the A4107 towards Treorchy at Croeserw. Turn left after about 2 miles into Blaengwynfi for the ground.

LLANELLI FC

Founded: 1896
Former Names: None
Nickname: 'Reds'
Ground: Stebonheath Park, Llanelli, Dyfed
Ground Telephone N°: (01554) 772973

Club Colours: Red shirts and shorts
Correspondence Address: Nigel Evans,
16 Tyshia Road, Llanelli SA15 1RW
Contact Telephone N°: (01554) 776760
Fax Number: (01554) 772973

GENERAL INFORMATION

Club Shop: None
Car Parking: At the ground
Coach Parking: At the ground
Nearest Railway Station: Llanelli (2 miles)
Nearest Bus Station: Llanelli (1 mile)
Nearest Police Station: Llanelli (1 mile)
Police Telephone N°: (01554) 772222

GROUND INFORMATION

Ground Capacity: 3,700
Seating Capacity: 700
Record Attendance: 18,000 vs Bristol Rovers
Pitch Size: 114 x 73 yards

ADMISSION INFO (2003/2004 PRICES)

Adult Standing: £4.00
Adult Seating: £4.00
Child Standing: £2.00
Child Seating: £2.00
Concessionary Standing: £2.00
Concessionary Seating: £2.00
Programme Price: £1.00

DISABLED SUPPORTERS INFORMATION

Wheelchairs: Accommodated
Disabled Toilets: Available
Contact Number: (01554) 772973

Web Site: www.llanelliafc.co.uk
E-mail: ridgewood.roberts40@virgin.net

Travelling Supporters' Information:
Routes: Take the M4 to Junction 48 and exit onto the A4138. Turn right at the traffic lights then left into Penallt Road for the ground; From the Station: Travel along Station Road to the Town Centre then turn right into Murray Street then into Stepney Place and James Street before turning right into Alban Road. Turn left into Bedford Street and then right into Evans Terrace for the ground.

LLANWERN FC

Founded: 1963
Former Names: Spencer Works FC
Nickname: None
Ground: Newport Stadium, Spytty Park,
Langland Way, Newport   NP19 4PT
Ground Tel. N°: (01633) 662262

Colours: Navy Blue shirts and shorts
Correspondence: Alan Watkins,
21 Traston Close, Newport   NP19 4TG
Contact Tel. N°: (01633) 671748

GENERAL INFORMATION
Car Parking: Space for 500 cars at the ground
Coach Parking: At the ground
Nearest Railway Station: Newport
Nearest Bus Station: Newport
Police Telephone N°: (01633) 244999

GROUND INFORMATION
Ground Capacity: 4,300
Seating Capacity: 1,200
Record Attendance: 3,721 (28/11/2001)
Pitch Size: 112 x 72 yards

ADMISSION INFO (2003/2004 PRICES)
Adult Standing: £2.00 (by programme)
Child Standing: Free of charge
Programme Price: £2.00 (includes admission)

DISABLED SUPPORTERS INFORMATION
Wheelchairs: Accommodated
Disabled Toilets: Yes
Contact: (01633) 671748

Travelling Supporters' Information:
Routes: Exit the M4 at Junction 24 and take the first exit at the roundabout, signposted 'Industrial Area'. After approximately a mile, turn left at the roundabout and then straight on at two further roundabouts before turning left and then left again into the stadium. The stadium is signposted from the M4 roundabout.

MAESTEG PARK AFC

Founded: 1945
Former Names: Maesteg Park Athletic FC
Nickname: 'The Park'
Ground: Tudor Park, St. David's Place, Park Estate, Maesteg, Mid Glamorgan
Ground Telephone Nº: (01656) 732029

Colours: Blue and White shirts with Blue shorts
Correspondence: D. Griffiths, 3 Padley's Close, Maesteg, Bridgend CF34 0TX
Contact Telephone Nº: (01656) 733000
Mobile Nº: (07855) 826270
Fax Number: (01656) 733000

GENERAL INFORMATION
Social Club Telephone Nº: (01656) 732029
Club Shop: Yes
Car Parking: At the ground
Coach Parking: At the ground
Nearest Railway Station: Maesteg (2½ miles)
Nearest Bus Station: Maesteg (2½ miles)
Nearest Police Station: Maesteg
Police Telephone Nº: (01656) 655555

GROUND INFORMATION
Ground Capacity: 2,000
Seating Capacity: None
Record Attendance: 1,000
Pitch Size: 112 x 78 yards

ADMISSION INFO (2003/2004 PRICES)
Adult Standing: £2.00 (by programme)
Child Standing: £1.00 (by programme)
Concessionary Standing: £1.00 (by programme)
Programme Price: Included in admission cost

DISABLED SUPPORTERS INFORMATION
Wheelchairs: Accommodated
Disabled Toilets: Available
Contact Number: (01656) 732029

Travelling Supporters' Information:
Routes: Leave the M4 at Junction 36 and take the A4063 to Maesteg. At the Cross Inn at Cwmfelin, turn left into the right hand lane up the steep hill. The ground is situated at the top of the hill on the left after passing the Red Cow pub on the right; On Foot: Take West Street from the Town Centre (turning off Commercial Street). Go up the hill then turn left at the junction. The ground is on the right.

NEATH FC

Founded: 1922
Former Names: National Oil Refineries FC, B.P. Llandarcy FC
Nickname: 'The Oilmen'
Ground: Llandarcy Park Sports Ground, Llandarcy, Neath, South Wales
Ground Telephone Nº: (01792) 812036

Colours: Yellow and Black shirts with Black shorts
Correspondence: John Harris, 24 Rowan Tree Close, Bryncoch, Neath SA10 7SJ
Contact Telephone Nº: (01639) 638882
Fax Number: (01639) 773288
Web Site: www.llandarcy.com
E-mail: terry.harvey@llandarcy.com

GENERAL INFORMATION
Social Club Telephone Nº: (01792) 812036
Club Shop: None
Car Parking: At the ground
Coach Parking: At the ground
Nearest Railway Station: Skewen (2 miles)
Nearest Bus Station: Neath
Nearest Police Station: Neath
Police Telephone Nº: (01639) 635321

GROUND INFORMATION
Ground Capacity: 1,500
Seating Capacity: 252
Record Attendance: Not known
Pitch Size: 110 x 75 yards

ADMISSION INFO (2003/2004 PRICES)
Adult Standing: £2.00
Adult Seating: £2.00
Child Standing: £1.50
Child Seating: £1.50
Programme Price: 50p

DISABLED SUPPORTERS INFORMATION
Wheelchairs: Accommodated
Disabled Toilets: Available
The Blind: No special facilities
Contact Number: (01792) 812036

Travelling Supporters' Information:
Routes: From the East: Exit the M4 at Junction 43, take the 1st exit at the roundabout and after about 150 yards follow signs for Llandarcy Park Sports Field to the right. Follow the road for the short distance to the ground; From the West: Exit the M4 at Junction 43 and take the 3rd exit at the roundabout. Then as above.

PONTARDAWE TOWN FC

Founded: 1947
Former Names: Pontardawe Athletic FC
Nickname: 'Ponty'
Ground: The Recreation Ground, Pontardawe, Glamorgan
Ground Telephone Nº: (01792) 862228

Colours: Black and White shirts with Black shorts
Correspondence: Kevin Stewart, 11 Church Street, Pontardawe, Swansea SA8 4JB
Contact Telephone Nº: (01792) 863233
Fax Number: None

GENERAL INFORMATION
Social Club: Gilberton Suite, Church Street, Pontardawe, West Glamorgan
Social Club Telephone Nº: (01792) 862230
Club Shop: None
Car Parking: At the ground
Coach Parking: At the ground
Nearest Railway Station: Neath (7 miles)
Nearest Bus Station: Pontardawe (¼ mile)
Nearest Police Station: Pontardawe (½ mile)
Police Telephone Nº: (01792) 456999

GROUND INFORMATION
Ground Capacity: 2,000
Seating Capacity: None
Record Attendance: 1,000 (vs Wrexham)
Pitch Size: 110 x 75 yards

ADMISSION INFO (2003/2004 PRICES)
Adult Standing: £2.50 (by programme)
Child Standing: £1.00 (by programme)
Programme Price: Included with admission

DISABLED SUPPORTERS INFORMATION
Wheelchairs: Accommodated
Disabled Toilets: None
Contact Number: (01792) 862228

Travelling Supporters' Information:
Routes: Exit the M4 at Junction 45 and take the A4067 to Pontardawe. Upon reaching Pontardawe, take the 1st exit at the roundabout across the river and at the next roundabout take the 3rd exit into Alloy Industrial Estate. The ground is situated at the far end of the Industrial Estate by a mini-roundabout.

TON PENTRE FC

Founded: 1935
Former Names: None
Nickname: 'Bulldogs'
Ground: Ynys Park, Ton Row, Ton Pentre, Rhondda, South Wales
Ground Telephone Nº: (01443) 442625

Club Colours: Red shirts and shorts
Correspondence: P.Willoughby, 37 Bailey Street, Ton Pentre, Rhondda   CF41 7EN
Contact Telephone Nº: (01443) 438281
Fax Number: None

GENERAL INFORMATION

Club Shop: Yes – at the ground
Car Parking: At the ground
Coach Parking: Llanfoist Street
Nearest Railway Station: Ton Pentre
Nearest Bus Station: Ton Pentre
Nearest Police Station: Ton Pentre
Police Telephone Nº: (01443) 434222

GROUND INFORMATION

Ground Capacity: 2,700
Seating Capacity: 530
Record Attendance: 6,000 vs Falmouth
Pitch Size: 110 x 70 yards

ADMISSION INFO (2003/2004 PRICES)

Adult Standing: £2.00
Adult Seating: £2.00
Child Standing: £1.00
Child Seating: £1.00
Concessionary Standing: £1.00
Concessionary Seating: £1.00
Programme Price: £1.00

DISABLED SUPPORTERS INFORMATION

Wheelchairs: Accommodated
Disabled Toilets: None
Contact Number: (01443) 442625

Travelling Supporters' Information:
Routes: Exit the M4 at Junction 34 and follow signs for Rhondda Valley and Treorchy. On reaching Pentre, turn left over the railway bridge and then first left again for the ground.

UWIC INTER CARDIFF FC

Founded: 1957
Former Names: Sully FC and Inter Cable Tel FC. Formed by the amalgamation of University of Wales Institute Cardiff FC and Inter Cardiff FC in 2000.
Nickname: 'The Archers'
Ground: Cyncoed College, Cyncoed Road, Cardiff, CF2 6XD
Ground Tel. Nº: (029) 2055-1111

Club Colours: Yellow shirts with Blue shorts
Correspondence: A.E. Evans, 132 Lake Road East, Cardiff   CF2 5NQ
Contact Telephone Nº: (029) 2074-7122
Fax Number: None
Web Site: www.uwicsu.co.uk/soccer
E-mail: clive.harry@lineone.net

GENERAL INFORMATION
Club Shop: None
Car Parking: At the ground
Coach Parking: At the ground
Nearest Railway Station: Heath Halt (1 mile)
Nearest Bus Station: City Centre
Nearest Police Station: Llanedeyrn, Cardiff
Police Telephone Nº: (029) 2022-2111

GROUND INFORMATION
Ground Capacity: 2,000
Seating Capacity: 150
Record Attendance: 1,350 vs Everton, August 1996
Pitch Size: 110 x 72 yards

ADMISSION INFO (2003/2004 PRICES)
Adult Standing: £1.50
Adult Seating: £1.50
Child Standing: £1.00
Child Seating: £1.00
Concessionary Standing: £1.00
Concessionary Seating: £1.00
Programme Price: Included with admission

DISABLED SUPPORTERS INFORMATION
Wheelchairs: Accommodated
Disabled Toilets: Available
Contact Number: (01633) 892119

Travelling Supporters' Information:
Routes: Exit the M4 at the Cardiff Gate Link. After about 2 miles take the A48, Eastern Avenue. Head towards Cardiff, passing the Post House Hotel on the right. At the Llanedeyrn Moat House Hotel interchange, take the 3rd exit and at the next roundabout take the 1st exit onto Llanedeyrn Road. After about 1 mile, take a right turn at the T-junction into Cyncoed Road and the ground is signposted on the right after about 1 mile.

Welsh Football

The independent voice of Welsh soccer

- *Unrivalled coverage of football in Wales*
- *Written by and for soccer enthusiasts*
- *published continuously for 12 years*
- *Eight issues per season (August – June)*

**Annual subscription cost =
£20 (including 2 free back issues)**

Apply to: Welsh Football, 57 Thornhill Road, Cardiff, CF14 6PE

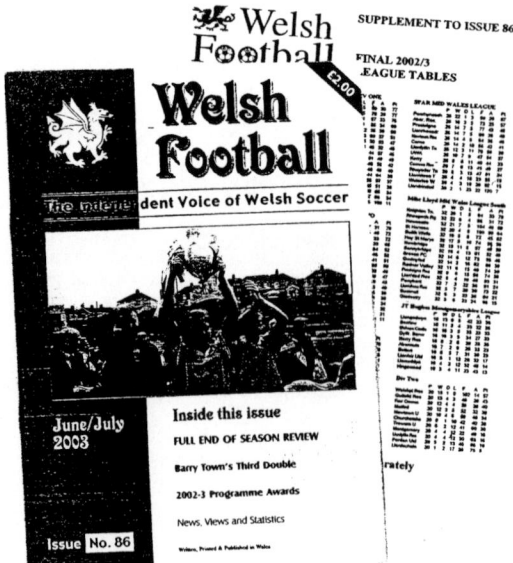

Every issue contains:

Welsh Premier scene
Welsh League news
Cymru Alliance news
Pyramid round-up
Club features
National team comment

New for 2003:
Up-to-the-minute
Statistics supplement

THE WELSH FOOTBALL LEAGUE

Address
Ken Tucker, 16 The Parade,
Merthyr Tydfil   CF47 0ET

Phone (01685) 723844   **Fax** (01685) 723844

Division Two Clubs for the 2003/2004 Season

Aberaman Athletic FC .... Page 70

AFC Llwydcoed .... Page 71

Ammanford AFC .... Page 72

Blaenrhondda AFC .... Page 73

Caldicot Town FC .... Page 74

Garden Village FC .... Page 75

Merthyr Saints FC .... Page 76

Milford United FC .... Page 77

Morriston Town FC .... Page 78

Newport YMCA FC .... Page 79

Penrhiwceiber Rangers FC .... Page 80

Pontyclun FC .... Page 81

Pontypridd Town FC .... Page 82

Porthcawl Town FC .... Page 83

Skewen Athletic FC .... Page 84

Taffs Well FC .... Page 85

Tredegar Town FC .... Page 86

Treharris Athletic FC .... Page 87

ABERAMAN ATHLETIC FC

Founded: 1892
Former Names: None
Nickname: 'Aber'
Ground: Aberaman Park, Aberaman, Aberdare, Mid Glamorgan
Ground Tel. Nº: None

Club Colours: Royal Blue shirts and shorts
Correspondence: Brian Fear, 28 Mostyn Street, Abercwmboi, Aberdare   CF44 6BB
Contact Tel. Nº: (01443) 472858
Fax Number: None
Web Site: www.aberamanafc.vze.com

GENERAL INFORMATION
Car Parking: At the ground
Coach Parking: At the ground
Nearest Railway Station: Aberdare
Nearest Bus Station: Aberdare
Nearest Police Station: Aberdare
Police Telephone Nº: (01685) 872461

GROUND INFORMATION
Ground Capacity: 2,000
Seating Capacity: 160
Record Attendance: 10,000 (during World War II)
Pitch Size: 115 x 75 yards

ADMISSION INFO (2003/2004 PRICES)
Adult Standing: £2.00 (by programme)
Adult Seating: £2.00 (by programme)
Child Standing: Free of charge
Child Seating: Free of charge
Programme Price: £2.00 (includes admission)

DISABLED SUPPORTERS INFORMATION
Wheelchairs: Accommodated
Disabled Toilets: None
Contact Number: (01443) 472858

Travelling Supporters' Information:
Routes: Exit the M4 at Junction 22 and take the A470 Northbound. Leave the A470 at signs for Mountain Ash and at the traffic lights on the railway bridge turn right. Proceed along this road for approximately 2 miles and the ground is situated on the right near the Kwik Save store.

AFC LLWYDCOED

Founded: 1948
Former Names: Llwydcoed Boys Club FC and Llwydcoed Welfare FC
Nickname: None
Ground: AFC Llwydcoed Welfare Ground, Merthyr Road, Llwydcoed, Aberdare   CF44 0YA
Ground Tel. N°: (01685) 873924

Colours: Black & White striped shirts, black shorts
Correspondence: David Evans, 25 Sycamore Close, Landare, Aberdare   CF44 8YD
Contact Tel. N°: (01685) 870422
Fax Number: (01685) 871541

GENERAL INFORMATION
Club Shop: c/o David Evans, 25 Sycamore Close, Landare
Car Parking: At the ground
Coach Parking: At the ground
Nearest Railway Station: Aberdare (2 miles)
Nearest Bus Station: Aberdare (2 miles)
Nearest Police Station: Trecynon

GROUND INFORMATION
Ground Capacity: 500
Seating Capacity: None
Record Attendance: Not known
Pitch Size: 110 x 65 yards

ADMISSION INFO (2003/2004 PRICES)
Adult Standing: £2.00 (by programme)
Child Standing: £2.00 (by programme)
Programme Price: £2.00 (includes admission)

DISABLED SUPPORTERS INFORMATION
Wheelchairs: Accommodated
Disabled Toilets: Available
Contact Number: (01685) 870422

Travelling Supporters' Information:
Routes: Leaving Neath on the A465, head towards Hirwaun. Take the 2nd exit at the 1st roundabout onto the Hirwaun Bypass then the 2nd exit at the next roundabout onto the A465 for Merthyr. At Baverstocks Hotel turn right onto the B4276 Llwydcoed/ Aberdare Road. The ground is situated on the left after approximately 1½ miles.

AMMANFORD AFC

Founded: 1991 (Formed with the amalgamation of Ammanford Town FC & Ammanford Athletic FC)
Former Names: Betws FC
Nickname: 'The Town'
Ground: Betws Sports Club, Rice Road, Betws, Ammanford, Dyfed
Ground Tel. Nº: (01269) 592407

Colours: Black & White striped shirts, Black shorts
Correspondence: W.J.Thomas, 154 Hendre Road, Capel Hendre, Ammanford SA18 3LE
Contact Tel. Nº: (01269) 843712
Fax Number: None

GENERAL INFORMATION
Club Shop: None
Car Parking: At the ground
Coach Parking: At the ground
Nearest Railway Station: Ammanford (½ mile)
Nearest Bus Station: Ammanford (½ mile)
Nearest Police Station: Ammanford
Police Telephone Nº: (01269) 592222

GROUND INFORMATION
Ground Capacity: 4,000
Seating Capacity: 450
Record Attendance: 4,000
Pitch Size: 105 x 75 yards

ADMISSION INFO (2003/2004 PRICES)
Adult Standing: £2.00 (by programme)
Adult Seating: £2.00 (by programme)
Child Standing: £2.00 (by programme)
Child Seating: £2.00 (by programme)
Programme Price: £2.00 (includes admission)

DISABLED SUPPORTERS INFORMATION
Wheelchairs: Accommodated
Disabled Toilets: None
Contact Number: (01269) 592407

Travelling Supporters' Information:
Routes: At the end of the M4 take the A483 then after approximately 5 miles turn right at traffic lights towards Betws. The ground is situated in Rice Road, Betws and is very hard to find!

BLAENRHONDDA AFC

Founded: 1934
Former Names: None
Nickname: None
Ground: Blaenrhondda Park, Blaenrhondda, Mid Glamorgan
Ground Tel. Nº: None

Colours: Blue shirts and shorts
Correspondence: Stephen A. Rumble, 85 Brynhyfryd Terrace, Ferndale, Rhondda, CF43 4HT
Contact Tel. Nº: (01443) 730141
Fax Number: None

GENERAL INFORMATION

Car Parking: Street parking but also the local School Yard for Cup Matches
Coach Parking: Street parking
Nearest Railway Station: Treherbert
Nearest Bus Station: Bus stop just outside the ground

GROUND INFORMATION

Ground Capacity: 2,500
Seating Capacity: None
Record Attendance: Approximately 1,000
Pitch Size: 105 x 78 yards

ADMISSION INFO (2003/2004 PRICES)

Adult Standing: £2.00
Child Standing: £1.00
Programme Price: Usually included with Adult admission

DISABLED SUPPORTERS INFORMATION

Wheelchairs: Accommodated
Disabled Toilets: None
Contact Number: (01443) 730141

Travelling Supporters' Information:
Routes: Take the A4061 to Treherbert and follow the road into Tynewydd then Blaenrhondda. The main road in Blaenrhondda is Brook Street and the entrance to the ground is directly opposite the Post Office (look for the Post Office sign on the wall).

CALDICOT TOWN FC

Founded: 1953
Former Names: Caldicot Playing Fields FC
Nickname: 'The Town'
Ground: Jubilee Way, Caldicot, Gwent
Ground Tel. Nº: (01291) 423519

Club Colours: White shirts with Black shorts
Correspondence: John Burrows, 12 Heron Road, Caldicot NP26 5RH
Contact Tel. Nº: (01291) 431529
Fax Number: None

GENERAL INFORMATION
Club Shop: None
Car Parking: At the ground
Coach Parking: At the ground
Nearest Railway Station: Caldicot
Nearest Bus Station: Caldicot Town Centre
Nearest Police Station: Caldicot
Police Telephone Nº: (01291) 430999

GROUND INFORMATION
Ground Capacity: 1,500
Seating Capacity: None
Record Attendance: 600
Pitch Size: 110 x 75 yards

ADMISSION INFO (2003/2004 PRICES)
Adult Standing: £2.00
Child Standing: £1.00
Programme Price: 50p

DISABLED SUPPORTERS INFORMATION
Wheelchairs: Accommodated
Disabled Toilets: None
Contact Number: (01291) 431529

Travelling Supporters' Information:
Routes: Exit the M4 at Junction 23(A) Magor Services. Turn right at the roundabout and follow signs for Caldicot. At the 3rd set of traffic lights turn left and follow the road past the Petrol station. The car park for the ground is on the right after 200 yards, the Clubhouse and ground itself is on the left.

GARDEN VILLAGE FC

Founded: 1922
Former Names: None
Nickname: 'Village'
Ground: Stafford Common, Victoria Road, Gorseinon, Swansea   SA4 3AB
Ground Telephone Nº: (01792) 894933

Club Colours: Black & White striped shirts, Black shorts
Correspondence: Clive Greenfield, 5 Maple Close, Peny Rhoel, Gorseinon, Swansea   SA4 4XL
Contact Telephone Nº: (01792) 517298
Fax Number: None
Web Site: www.eteamz.com/GardenVillageafc

GENERAL INFORMATION
Club Shop: At the ground on matchdays only
Car Parking: At the ground
Coach Parking: At the ground
Nearest Railway Station: Gowerton (1 mile)
Nearest Bus Station: Gorseinon
Nearest Police Station: Gorseinon
Police Telephone Nº: (01792) 456999

GROUND INFORMATION
Ground Capacity: 2,000
Seating Capacity: None
Record Attendance: Not known
Pitch Size: 110 x 70 yards

ADMISSION INFO (2003/2004 PRICES)
Adult Standing: £2.00
Child Standing: Free of charge
Programme Price: 50p

DISABLED SUPPORTERS INFORMATION
Wheelchairs: Accommodated
Disabled Toilets: None
Contact Number: (01792) 894933

Travelling Supporters' Information:
Routes: Exit the M4 at Junction 47 and follow signs for Swansea. Take the 2nd exit at the first roundabout signposted Llanelli and continue for one mile. Go straight on at the next roundabout, then take the 3rd exit at the following roundabout. Follow the road for ½ mile and the ground is situated on the right.

MERTHYR SAINTS FC

Founded: During the 1950s
Former Names: Hoover Sports FC
Nickname: 'Saints'
Ground: ICI Pavilion, Bryniau Road, Pant, Merthyr Tydfil
Ground Tel. No: (01685) 386140

Club Colours: Blue shirts and shorts
Correspondence: Ron Jones, 6 Brunswick Street, Merthyr Tydfil CF47 8SB
Contact Tel. No: (01685) 377871
Fax Number: None

GENERAL INFORMATION
Club Shop: At the ground
Car Parking: At the ground
Coach Parking: None
Nearest Railway Station: Merthyr Tydfil (1½ miles)
Nearest Bus Station: Pant (adjacent)
Nearest Police Station: Dowlais

GROUND INFORMATION
Ground Capacity: 1,000
Seating Capacity: None
Record Attendance: 200
Pitch Size: 99 x 77 yards

ADMISSION INFO (2003/2004 PRICES)
Adult Standing: £2.50
Child Standing: Free of charge
Programme Price: 50p

DISABLED SUPPORTERS INFORMATION
Wheelchairs: Accommodated
Disabled Toilets: None
Contact Number: (01685) 377871

Travelling Supporters' Information:
Routes: Take the 1st exit off the A465 'Heads of the Valleys Road' signposted for Prince Charles Hospital and head for the Brecon Mountain Railway Park. The ground is in Bryniau Road, adjacent to the Pant Industrial Park.

MILFORD UNITED FC

Founded: 1885
Former Names: None
Nickname: 'The Robins'
Ground: Marble Hall Road, Milford Haven, Pembrokeshire
Ground Telephone Nº: (01646) 693691

Club Colours: Red shirts with White shorts
Correspondence: Brian Goodwin, 8 Penygraig Drive, Templeton, Narberth   SA67 8SU
Contact Telephone Nº: (01834) 860953
Mobile Nº: (07733) 192573

GENERAL INFORMATION
Social Club Telephone Nº: (01646) 693691
Club Shop: At the ground
Car Parking: At the ground
Coach Parking: At the ground
Nearest Railway Station: Milford Haven
Nearest Bus Station: Milford Haven (1½ miles)
Nearest Police Station: Milford Haven
Police Telephone Nº: –

GROUND INFORMATION
Ground Capacity: 4,000
Seating Capacity: 400
Record Attendance: Approximately 4,000 (1950's)
Pitch Size: 108 x 75 yards

ADMISSION INFO (2003/2004 PRICES)
Adult Standing: £1.50
Adult Seating: £1.50
Child Standing: Free of charge
Child Seating: Free of charge
Programme Price: 50p

DISABLED SUPPORTERS INFORMATION
Wheelchairs: Accommodated
Disabled Toilets: None
Contact Number: (01646) 693691

Travelling Supporters' Information:
Routes: Take the A4076 from Haverfordwest. Upon entering Milford Haven, turn right into Marble Hall Road and the first cross-roads. The ground is situated about 300 yards on the left.

MORRISTON TOWN FC

Founded: 1926
Former Names: Grove Mission FC and Midland Athletic FC
Nickname: None
Ground: Dingle Road, Morriston, Swansea
Ground Telephone Nº: (01792) 702033

Club Colours: Red shirts and shorts
Correspondence: David Bennett, 51 Severn Road, Clase, Morriston, Swansea SA6 7LQ
Contact Tel. Nº: (01792) 791713
Fax Number: None

GENERAL INFORMATION
Car Parking: At the ground
Coach Parking: At the ground
Nearest Railway Station: Swansea
Nearest Bus Station: Swansea
Nearest Police Station: Morriston
Police Telephone Nº: (01792) 771294

GROUND INFORMATION
Ground Capacity: 1,000
Seating Capacity: None
Record Attendance: Approximately 600 vs Swansea
Pitch Size: 104 x 74 yards

ADMISSION INFO (2003/2004 PRICES)
Adult Standing: £2.00 (by programme)
Child Standing: Free of charge
Concessionary Standing: £1.00 (by programme)
Programme Price: Included with admission

DISABLED SUPPORTERS INFORMATION
Wheelchairs: Accommodated
Disabled Toilets: None
Contact Number: (01792) 791713

Travelling Supporters' Information:
Routes: Exit the M4 at Junction 45 for Swansea and take the 2nd exit at the roundabout bearing left. The ground is situated ½ mile along this road on the right hand side behind the houses.

NEWPORT YMCA AFC

Founded: 1971
Former Names: Pill YMCA and Central YMCA
Nickname: None
Ground: Mendalgief Road, Newport
Ground Tel. Nº: (01633) 266872

Colours: Yellow and Blue shirts with Blue shorts
Correspondence: Michael James,
2 Gaer Park Parade, Newport   NP20 3NX
Contact Tel. Nº: (01633) 662571
Fax Number: None

GENERAL INFORMATION
Club Shop: None
Car Parking: At the ground
Coach Parking: Adjacent to the ground
Nearest Railway Station: Newport Central
Nearest Bus Station: Newport
Nearest Police Station: Cardiff Road, Newport
Police Telephone Nº: (01633) 244999

GROUND INFORMATION
Ground Capacity: 1,000
Seating Capacity: None
Record Attendance: Not known
Pitch Size: 110 x 65 yards

ADMISSION INFO (2003/2004 PRICES)
Adult Standing: £2.00
Child Standing: Free of charge
Programme Price: Included with admission

DISABLED SUPPORTERS INFORMATION
Wheelchairs: Accommodated
Disabled Toilets: Available
Contact Number: (01633) 266872

Travelling Supporters' Information:
Routes: Exit the M4 at Junction 28 and take Newport Road to the next roundabout. At the roundabout take the 2nd exit signposted for the Docks and follow the road under the railway bridge to the T-junction. Turn right and the ground is situated on the right hand side after 200 yards.

PENRHIWCEIBER RANGERS FC

Founded: 1961
Former Names: Penrhiwceiber Welfare FC
Nickname: None
Ground: Glasbrook Field, Glasbrook Terrace, Mountain Ash, Mid Glamorgan
Ground Telephone Nº: None

Club Colours: Red shirts and shorts
Correspondence: J.Dudley, 131 Abercynon Road, Abercynon CF45 4NE
Contact Telephone Nº: (01443) 741433
Fax Number: None

GENERAL INFORMATION
Club Shop: None
Car Parking: Street parking
Coach Parking: Street parking
Nearest Railway Station: Penrhiwceiber (400 yards)
Nearest Bus Station: Penrhiwceiber
Nearest Police Station: Mountain Ash
Police Telephone Nº: –

GROUND INFORMATION
Ground Capacity: 3,000
Seating Capacity: 300
Record Attendance: Not known
Pitch Size: 110 x 72 yards

ADMISSION INFO (2003/2004 PRICES)
Adult Standing: £1.00
Adult Seating: £1.00
Child Standing: 50p
Child Seating: 50p
Concessionary Standing: 50p
Concessionary Seating: 50p
Programme Price: 50p

DISABLED SUPPORTERS INFORMATION
Wheelchairs: Accommodated
Disabled Toilets: None
Contact Number: (01443) 741433

Travelling Supporters' Information:
Routes: Exit the M4 at Junction 32 and follow signs for Merthyr (A470). Carry along the A470 to the end and exit at the roundabout for Abercynon West. Pass through Abercynon and after 1½ miles, the ground is on the right.

PONTYCLUN FC

Founded: 1896
Former Names: None
Nickname: 'The Clun'
Ground: Ivor Park, Cowbridge Road, Pontyclun
Clubhouse Tel. N°: (01443) 222182

Club Colours: Blue shirts with Black shorts
Correspondence: Peter Shilton, 16 Castan Road, Pontyclun CF72 9EH
Contact Tel. N°: (01443) 239658
Fax Number: None

GENERAL INFORMATION
Social Club Telephone N°: (01443) 222182
Club Shop: None
Car Parking: At the ground
Coach Parking: At the ground
Nearest Railway Station: Pontyclun (½ mile)
Nearest Bus Station: Talbot Green (2 miles)
Nearest Police Station: Talbot Green

GROUND INFORMATION
Ground Capacity: 1,000
Seating Capacity: None
Record Attendance: Approximately 500
Pitch Size: 105 x 72 yards

ADMISSION INFO (2003/2004 PRICES)
Adult Standing: £2.00 (by programme)
Child Standing: £1.00 (by programme)
Programme Price: Included with admission

DISABLED SUPPORTERS INFORMATION
Wheelchairs: Accommodated
Disabled Toilets: None
Contact Number: (01443) 239658

Travelling Supporters' Information:
Routes: Exit the M4 at Junction 34, take the A4119 towards Llantrisant and follow signs for Cowbridge. Pass Leekes DIY store on the left and pass through Pontyclun. The ground is on the left before the Ivor Arms public house.

PONTYPRIDD TOWN AFC

Founded: 1895
Former Names: Ynysbwl FC
Nickname: 'The Dragons'
Ground: Ynysangharad War Memorial Park, Pontypridd
Ground Tel. Nº: (01443) 486571

Colours: Black and White shirts with Black shorts
Correspondence: Alf Germain, 1 Birdsfield Cottage, Graig, Pontypridd   CF37 1LE
Contact Tel. Nº: (01443) 407868
Fax Number: None

GENERAL INFORMATION
Club Shop: None
Car Parking: Street parking only
Coach Parking: Street parking only
Nearest Railway Station: Pontypridd (½ mile)
Nearest Bus Station: Pontypridd (½ mile)
Nearest Police Station: Pontypridd
Police Telephone Nº: (01443) 485351

GROUND INFORMATION
Ground Capacity: 2,000
Seating Capacity: 150
Record Attendance: Not known
Pitch Size: 110 x 70 yards

ADMISSION INFO (2003/2004 PRICES)
Adult Standing: £1.50 (by programme)
Adult Seating: £1.50 (by programme)
Child Standing: Free of charge when with a paying adult
Child Seating: Free of charge when with a paying adult
Programme Price: £1.50 (includes admission)

DISABLED SUPPORTERS INFORMATION
Wheelchairs: Accommodated
Disabled Toilets: Available
Contact Number: (07786) 523577

Travelling Supporters' Information:
Routes: Take the A470 dual carriageway and exit at the Ynysybwl turn-off. The ground is situated adjacent to the A470 northbound in Ynysangharad War Memorial Park.

PORTHCAWL TOWN FC

Founded: 1947
Former Names: None
Nickname: 'Seasiders'
Ground: Locks Lane, Porthcawl, South Wales
Ground Tel. Nº: (01656) 784804

Club Colours: Navy Blue shirts and shorts
Correspondence: Steve Harris, 18 Mary Street, Porthcawl CF36 3YA
Contact Tel. Nº: (01656) 786946
Fax Number: (01656) 785900

GENERAL INFORMATION
Club Shop: None
Car Parking: 100 spaces available at the ground
Coach Parking: At the ground
Nearest Railway Station: Bridgend (6 miles)
Nearest Bus Station: Bridgend (6 miles)
Nearest Police Station: John Street, Porthcawl
Police Telephone Nº: (01656) 655555

GROUND INFORMATION
Ground Capacity: 1,000
Seating Capacity: None
Record Attendance: 2,000
Pitch Size: 100 x 67 yards

ADMISSION INFO (2003/2004 PRICES)
Adult Standing: £1.00 (by programme)
Child Standing: Free of charge
Programme Price: £1.00 (includes admission)

DISABLED SUPPORTERS INFORMATION
Wheelchairs: Accommodated
Disabled Toilets: None
Contact Number: (01656) 788038

Travelling Supporters' Information:
Routes: Exit the M4 at Junction 37 and take the first exit at the roundabout (signposted Porthcawl). Continue straight on at the 2nd roundabout then take the 3rd exit at the next roundabout onto the A4229. Take the 3rd exit at the next roundabout into Falmer Road travelling uphill. The road then bends sharply to the left and becomes Mallard Way. Continue along this road and turn first left into Locks Lane. The ground is then on the left.

SKEWEN ATHLETIC FC

Founded: 1932
Former Names: Garthmoor FC and Neath Athletic FC
Nickname: None
Ground: Tennant Park, Skewen, Near Neath
Ground Tel. Nº: None

Club Colours: Sky Blue shirts with White shorts
Correspondence: A.J.Melding, 15 Bosworth Road, Skewen, Neath   SA10 6BU
Contact Tel. Nº: (01792) 812431
Fax Number: None

GENERAL INFORMATION
Club Shop: None
Car Parking: 100 spaces available at the ground
Coach Parking: 4 spaces available at the ground
Nearest Railway Station: Neath
Nearest Bus Station: Neath
Nearest Police Station: Skewen

GROUND INFORMATION
Ground Capacity: 2,000
Seating Capacity: None
Record Attendance: Not known
Pitch Size: 100 x 65 yards

ADMISSION INFO (2003/2004 PRICES)
Adult Standing: £2.00 (by programme)
Child Standing: £2.00 (by programme)
Programme Price: £2.00 (includes admission)

DISABLED SUPPORTERS INFORMATION
Wheelchairs: Accommodated
Disabled Toilets: Available
Contact Number: (01792) 812431

Travelling Supporters' Information:
Routes: Exit the M4 at Junction 43 and take the first turning on the left before turning immediately right. Go under the bridge then take the second exit on the left before turning right at the T-Junction. Take the first turning on the left and then first left again before following the road into the ground.

TAFFS WELL FC

Founded: 1947
Former Names: None
Nickname: 'The Taffs'
Ground: Rhiw Dda'r, Parish Road, Taffs Well, Mid Glamorgan
Ground Tel. N°: (029) 2081-1080

Club Colours: Yellow shirts with Black shorts
Correspondence: Norma Samuel, 103 Hillside Park, Taffs Well, Cardiff
Contact Tel. N°: (029) 2081-3020
Fax Number: None

GENERAL INFORMATION
Club Shop: None
Car Parking: At the ground
Coach Parking: At the ground
Nearest Railway Station: Taffs Well
Nearest Bus Station: Cardiff
Nearest Police Station: Taffs Well

GROUND INFORMATION
Ground Capacity: 3,000
Seating Capacity: None
Record Attendance: 631
Pitch Size: 110 x 70 yards

ADMISSION INFO (2003/2004 PRICES)
Adult Standing: £3.00
Child Standing: Free of charge
Programme Price: £1.00

DISABLED SUPPORTERS INFORMATION
Wheelchairs: Accommodated
Disabled Toilets: None
Contact Number: (029) 2081-3020

Travelling Supporters' Information:
Routes: Exit the M4 at Junction 32 and take the A470 to Merthyr. Then follow the B4052 to Taffs Well, pass through the village and over the 2nd railway bridge before taking the next turning on the right for the ground.

TREDEGAR TOWN FC

Founded: 1980
Former Names: None
Nickname: 'Town'
Ground: Tredegar Recreation Ground, Tredegar, Gwent
Ground Tel. N°: (01495) 711791

Colours: Red, White and Black shirts, Black shorts
Correspondence: Riley Gray, 7 Gladstone Place, Tredegar, Gwent   NP22 4LG
Contact Tel. N°: (01495) 724582
Fax Number: None
Note: The club plan to move to the Leisure Centre Stadium later in the season

GENERAL INFORMATION
Social Club Telephone N°: (01495) 711791
Club Shop: None
Car Parking: At the ground
Coach Parking: At the ground
Nearest Railway Station: Rhymney (1 mile)
Nearest Bus Station: Tredegar
Nearest Police Station: Tredegar

GROUND INFORMATION
Ground Capacity: 1,000
Seating Capacity: None
Record Attendance: Approximately 300
Pitch Size: 120 x 77 yards

ADMISSION INFO (2003/2004 PRICES)
Adult Standing: £2.00
Adult Seating: £2.00
Child Standing: £1.00
Child Seating: £1.00
Programme Price: Included in admission price

DISABLED SUPPORTERS INFORMATION
Wheelchairs: Accommodated
Disabled Toilets: Available
Contact Number: (01495) 724582

Travelling Supporters' Information:
Routes: From the South: Take the A4048 to Tredegar. When entering Tedegar, take the first turning on the left onto the bypass then turn left at the roundabout. Pass Tredegar Comprehensive School and take the first left at the top of the hill for the ground; From the West: Take the A465 Heads of the Valleys road and then the A4048 to Tredegar.

TREHARRIS ATHLETIC FC

Founded: 1889
Former Names: None
Nickname: 'The Lilywhites'
Ground: Athletic Ground, Spencer Place, Treharris, Mid Glamorgan
Ground Tel. N°: None

Club Colours: Blue and Yellow shirts with Blue shorts
Correspondence: Mike Casey, 10 Windsor Road, Edwardsville, Treharris CF46 5NP
Contact Tel. N°: (01443) 411153
Fax Number: None

GENERAL INFORMATION

Club Shop: None
Car Parking: Limited number of spaces at the ground
Coach Parking: None
Nearest Railway Station: Quakers Yard (1½ miles)
Nearest Bus Station: Treharris Square
Nearest Police Station: Treharris
Police Telephone N°: (01443) 412455

GROUND INFORMATION

Ground Capacity: 1,500
Seating Capacity: None
Record Attendance: Not known
Pitch Size: 105 x 60 yards

ADMISSION INFO (2003/2004 PRICES)

Adult Standing: £2.00
Child Standing: £1.00
Senior Citizen Standing: £1.50
Programme Price: Included in admission price

DISABLED SUPPORTERS INFORMATION

Wheelchairs: Accommodated
Disabled Toilets: None
Contact Number: (01443) 472858

Travelling Supporters' Information:
Routes: Take the A470 from Cardiff or Merthyr and follow signs for Treharris. Once in Treharris, the ground is situated by the Fire Station.

Supporters' Guides & Other Titles

This top-selling series has been published annually since 1982 and contains 2002/2003 Season's results and tables, Directions, Photographs, Phone numbers, Parking information, Admission details, Disabled information and much more.

THE SUPPORTERS' GUIDE TO PREMIER & FOOTBALL LEAGUE CLUBS 2004

The 20th edition featuring all Premiership and Football League clubs. *Price £6.99*

THE SUPPORTERS' GUIDE TO NON-LEAGUE FOOTBALL 2004

The 11th edition featuring all Conference, Unibond Premier, Rymans Premier and Dr. Martens Premier clubs. *Price £6.99*

THE SUPPORTERS' GUIDE TO SCOTTISH FOOTBALL 2004

The 11th edition featuring all Scottish League and Highland League clubs. *Price £6.99*

THE SUPPORTERS' GUIDE TO FOOTBALL PROGRAMMES 2004

Produced in conjunction with *Programme Monthly* magazine, this book contains an appraisal of the programmes of all 92 Premier and Football League Clubs during the 2002/2003 Season. *Price £6.99*

FOOTBALL LEAGUE TABLES 1888-2003

The 6th edition contains every Football League, Premier League, Scottish League and Scottish Premier League Final Table from 1888-2003 together with Cup Final information. *Price £9.99*

NON-LEAGUE FOOTBALL TABLES 1889-2003

The 2nd edition contains final tables for the Connference, it's 3 feeder Leagues and the 4 North Western Leagues in England (which were not included in the 1st edition). *Price £9.95*

These books are available UK & Surface post free from –

Soccer Books Limited (Dept. SBL)
72 St. Peter's Avenue
Cleethorpes
N.E. Lincolnshire
DN35 8HU

THE WELSH FOOTBALL LEAGUE

Address

Ken Tucker, 16 The Parade,
Merthyr Tydfil   CF47 0ET

Phone (01685) 723844   **Fax** (01685) 723844

Division Three Clubs for the 2003/2004 Season

AFC Rhondda .... Page 90

Albion Rovers FC .... Page 91

Bryntirion Athletic FC .... Page 92

Caerau Ely FC .... Page 93

Chepstow Town FC .... Page 94

Cwmamman United FC .... Page 95

Fields Park Pontllanfraith FC .... Page 96

Goytre FC (Gwent) .... Page 97

Llantwit Fardre FC .... Page 98

Newcastle Emlyn FC .... Page 99

Pentwyn Dynamos FC .... Page 100

Pontlottyn Blast Furnace FC .... Page 101

Porth Tywyn Suburbs FC .... Page 102

Risca & Gelli United AFC .... Page 103

Seven Sisters AFC .... Page 104

Tillery FC .... Page 105

Treowen Stars FC .... Page 106

Troedyrhiw FC .... Page 107

AFC RHONDDA

Founded: 1950
Former Names: Beatus United FC and AFC Porth
Nickname: 'Black Dragons'
Ground: Dinas Park, Dinas, Porth, Rhondda, Mid Glamorgan
Ground Telephone N°: (01443) 688073

Colours: Maroon & Blue shirts with Blue shorts
Correspondence: Eric Thomas, 28 Trealaw Road, Tonypandy, Rhondda CF40 2NS
Contact Telephone N°: (01443) 442395
Fax Number: (01443) 442345

GENERAL INFORMATION
Social Club Telephone N°: (01443) 688073
Club Shop: Yes
Car Parking: At the ground
Coach Parking: At the ground
Nearest Railway Station: Dinas
Nearest Bus Station: Dinas
Nearest Police Station: Porth
Police Telephone N°: –

GROUND INFORMATION
Ground Capacity: 2,000
Seating Capacity: 200
Record Attendance: 1,700
Pitch Size: 110 x 83 yards

ADMISSION INFO (2003/2004 PRICES)
Adult Standing: £2.00
Adult Seating: £2.00
Child Standing: 50p
Child Seating: 50p
Concessionary Standing: 50p
Concessionary Seating: 50p
Programme Price: Included with admission

DISABLED SUPPORTERS INFORMATION
Wheelchairs: Accommodated
Disabled Toilets: Available
Contact Number: (01443) 688073

Travelling Supporters' Information:
Routes: Exit the M4 at Junction 32 and take the A470 towards Merthyr Tydfil. Leave the A470 at signs for Pontypridd (Rhondda Valley). On reaching Porth follow signs for Dinas/Tonypandy and the ground is on the right after 3 miles.

ALBION ROVERS FC

Founded: 1937
Former Names: None
Nickname: 'The Reds'
Ground: Newport Stadium, Spytty Park, Langland Way, Newport   NP19 4PT
Ground Tel. Nº: (01633) 662262

Colours: Red & White striped shirts with Red shorts
Correspondence: Mrs Karen Donovan,
15 Aspen Way, Malpas, Newport   NP20 6LB
Contact Tel. Nº: (01633) 770511

GENERAL INFORMATION
Car Parking: Space for 500 cars at the ground
Coach Parking: At the ground
Nearest Railway Station: Newport
Nearest Bus Station: Newport
Police Telephone Nº: (01633) 244999

GROUND INFORMATION
Ground Capacity: 4,300
Seating Capacity: 1,200
Record Attendance: 3,721 (28/11/2001)
Pitch Size: 112 x 72 yards

ADMISSION INFO (2003/2004 PRICES)
Adult Standing: £2.00
Child Standing: £1.00
Programme Price: 50p

DISABLED SUPPORTERS INFORMATION
Wheelchairs: Accommodated
Disabled Toilets: Yes
Contact Number: (01633) 770511

Travelling Supporters' Information:
Routes: Exit the M4 at Junction 24 and take the first exit at the roundabout, signposted 'Industrial Area'. After approximately a mile, turn left at the roundabout and then straight on at two further roundabouts before turning left and then left again into the stadium. The stadium is signposted from the M4 roundabout.

BRYNTYRION ATHLETIC FC

Founded: 1956
Former Names: None
Nickname: 'Athletic'
Ground: Llangewydd Road, Bridgend   CF31 4JU
Ground Tel. Nº: (01656) 652702

Club Colours: Blue shirts and shorts
Correspondence: Vic Carpenter, 23A Heol Gadlys, Litchard, Bridgend   CF31 1PD
Contact Tel. Nº: (01656) 664268
Fax Number: (01656) 652703

GENERAL INFORMATION
Club Shop: None
Car Parking: Approximately 60 spaces at the ground
Coach Parking: At the ground
Nearest Railway Station: Bridgend
Nearest Bus Station: Bridgend
Nearest Police Station: Bridgend
Police Telephone Nº: (01656) 655555

GROUND INFORMATION
Ground Capacity: 1,000
Seating Capacity: None
Record Attendance: Not known
Pitch Size: 120 x 87 yards

ADMISSION INFO (2003/2004 PRICES)
Adult Standing: £2.00
Child Standing: Free of charge
Programme Price: Included in the cost of admission

DISABLED SUPPORTERS INFORMATION
Wheelchairs: Accommodated
Disabled Toilets: Available
Contact Number: (01656) 664268

Travelling Supporters' Information:
Routes: Exit the M4 at Junction 35 and proceed left along the A48 towards Bridgend. Go straight on at 4 roundabouts (including a mini-roundabout) and continue for approximately 2 miles down the hill before turning left at the next roundabout, signposted for Laleston. Pass through the village and, after leaving the village, take the 1st turning on the left followed by the second left. Take the first left and go up the hill before turning right at the T-Junction. Then take the first left for the ground.

CAERAU ELY AFC

Founded: 1955
Former Names: None
Nickname: None
Ground: Cwrt-yr-Ala, Ely, Cardiff
Ground Tel. N°: None

Club Colours: Blue shirts with Black shorts
Correspondence: John Jarvis,
326 Cowbridge Road West, Ely, Cardiff
Contact Tel. N°: (029) 2059-1969
Fax Number: None

GENERAL INFORMATION
Car Parking: At the ground
Coach Parking: At the ground
Nearest Railway Station: Cardiff Central
Nearest Bus Station: Cardiff Central
Nearest Police Station: Canton

GROUND INFORMATION
Ground Capacity: 1,000
Seating Capacity: 50
Record Attendance: Not known
Pitch Size: 105 x 72 yards

ADMISSION INFO (2003/2004 PRICES)
Adult Standing: £1.00 (by programme)
Adult Seating: £1.00 (by programme)
Child Standing: Free of charge
Child Seating: Free of charge
Programme Price: Included with admission

DISABLED SUPPORTERS INFORMATION
Wheelchairs: Accommodated
Disabled Toilets: None
Contact Number: (029) 2059-1969

Travelling Supporters' Information:
Routes: Exit the M4 at Junction 33, take the A4232 link road and pass the minor exit for the Museum of Welsh Life. Leave at the next exit (Culverhouse Cross) and take the 1st exit at the roundabout towards Cardiff on the A48. After approximately ½ mile, turn right into Heol Trelai, then right again into Caerau Lane then first left into Cwrt-yr-Ala Lane. Follow this road under the flyover for the ground.

CHEPSTOW TOWN FC

Founded: 1878
Former Names: None
Nickname: None
Ground: Newport Road, Chepstow
Ground Telephone Nº: (01291) 629220

Colours: Blue & White quartered shirts, Blue shorts
Correspondence: Robert Stait, 53 Raglan Way, Bulwark, Chepstow   NP16 5QP
Contact Tel. Nº: (01291) 629731
Fax Number: None

GENERAL INFORMATION
Car Parking: At the ground
Coach Parking: At the ground
Nearest Railway Station: Chepstow (1 mile)
Nearest Bus Station: Chepstow (½ mile)
Nearest Police Station: Chepstow

GROUND INFORMATION
Ground Capacity: 1,000
Seating Capacity: 70
Record Attendance: Approximately 400
Pitch Size: 110 x 65 yards

ADMISSION INFO (2003/2004 PRICES)
Adult Standing: 50p (by programme)
Child Standing: Free of charge
Programme Price: Included with admission

DISABLED SUPPORTERS INFORMATION
Wheelchairs: Accommodated
Disabled Toilets: Available
Contact Number: (01291) 629731

Travelling Supporters' Information:
Routes: Exit the M48 at Junction 2, take the A466 towards Chepstow then turn right at the roundabout onto the A48. The ground is situated on the right after 300 yards opposite Chepstow Hotel.

CWMAMMAN UNITED AFC

Founded: 1976
Former Names: Glanamman FC
Nickname: None
Ground: Grenig Park, Cwmamman, Nr. Ammanford
Ground Tel. N°: (01269) 823107
Web Site: www.cwmamman-afc.co.uk

Club Colours: Blue and Black shirts with Black shorts
Correspondence: Alun Rees, 81 Parc Brynrhos, Glanamman, Ammanford SA18 1JE
Contact Tel. N°: (01269) 824364
Fax Number: (01269) 851096

GENERAL INFORMATION
Social Club Telephone N°: (01269) 823107
Club Shop: None
Car Parking: Approximately 40 spaces at the ground
Coach Parking: Approximately 2 spaces at the ground
Nearest Railway Station: Neath (14 miles)
Nearest Bus Station: Ammanford (2½ miles)
Nearest Police Station: Ammanford
Police Telephone N°: (01269) 592222

GROUND INFORMATION
Ground Capacity: 1,000
Seating Capacity: 150
Record Attendance: Approximately 250
Pitch Size: 99 x 69 yards

ADMISSION INFO (2003/2004 PRICES)
Adult Standing: £2.00
Child Standing: Free of charge
Programme Price: Included in the cost of admission

DISABLED SUPPORTERS INFORMATION
Wheelchairs: Accommodated
Disabled Toilets: Available
Contact Number: (01269) 824364

Travelling Supporters' Information:
Routes: Take the M4 then exit at the service area at Portabraham. Take the 2nd left heading for Ammanford (5 miles). On reaching Ammanford go straight through the lights towards Glanamman (3 mile). The ground is 1 mile after the Glanamman sign.

FIELDS PARK PONTLLANFRAITH FC

Founded: Reformed 1964
Former Names: Fields Park FC
Nickname: None
Ground: Islwyn Park, Pontllanfraith, Blackwood, Gwent
Ground Tel. Nº: (01495) 224512

Colours: Royal Blue shirts and shorts
Correspondence: John Bray, 113 Park Place, Gilfach, Bargoed   CF81 8LY
Contact Tel. Nº: (01443) 832513
Fax Number: None

GENERAL INFORMATION
Club Shop: None
Car Parking: At the ground
Coach Parking: At the ground
Nearest Railway Station: Newport (12 miles)
Nearest Bus Station: Blackwood
Nearest Police Station: Pontllanfraith
Police Telephone Nº: –

GROUND INFORMATION
Ground Capacity: 2,000
Seating Capacity: None
Record Attendance: Approximately 3,000
Pitch Size: 110 x 60 yards

ADMISSION INFO (2003/2004 PRICES)
Adult Standing: £2.00 (by programme)
Child Standing: £2.00 (by programme)
Programme Price: Included with admission

DISABLED SUPPORTERS INFORMATION
Wheelchairs: Accommodated
Disabled Toilets: None
Contact Number: (01443) 832513

Travelling Supporters' Information:
Routes: Exit the M4 at Junction 28 and take the A467 then the A4048 and A472 to Pontllanfraith. Upon reaching Pontllanfraith, follow signs for Springfield Estate. Turn sharp right at the traffic lights by Plough Inn and the ground is ¼ mile on the right off Llanarth Road.

GOYTRE FC (GWENT)

Founded: 1902
Former Names: None
Nickname: None
Ground: Plough Road, Penperlleni, Monmouthshire
Ground Tel. N°: None

Colours: Red & Black striped shirts with Black shorts
Correspondence: David Melmoth, Carrig-y-Melin, School Lane, Penperlleni, Near Pontypool NP4 0AH
Contact Tel. N°: (01873) 880569
Fax Number: None
Web Site: www.goytrefc.co.uk

GENERAL INFORMATION
Car Parking: At the ground
Coach Parking: At the ground
Nearest Railway Station: Abergavenny (4 miles)
Nearest Bus Station: Abergavenny
Nearest Police Station: Pontypool

GROUND INFORMATION
Ground Capacity: 1,000
Seating Capacity: 50
Record Attendance: Approximately 400 vs Newport County
Pitch Size: 110 x 65 yards

ADMISSION INFO (2003/2004 PRICES)
Adult Standing: £1.00 (by programme)
Child Standing: £1.00 (by programme)
Programme Price: Included with admission)

DISABLED SUPPORTERS INFORMATION
Wheelchairs: Accommodated
Disabled Toilets: Available
Contact Number: (01873) 880569

Travelling Supporters' Information:
Routes: Exit the M4 at Junction 25A and take the A4042 to Pontypool. Continue past Pontypool towards Abergavenny and turn right into the village of Penperlleni by the Goytre Arms. Follow the road then turn first right after the railway bridge and the ground is situated about ½ mile along on the left.

LLANTWIT FARDRE FC

Founded: 1958
Former Names: Llantwit Fardre Juniors FC
Nickname: None
Ground: Tonteg Park, Llantwit Fardre, Pontypridd
Ground Telephone Nº: None
Club Colours: Sky Blue shirts with Navy Blue shorts

Correspondence: Gary Lord, 4 Birchwood Drive, Mountain View, Tonyrefail, South Wales
Contact Tel. Nº: (01443) 671971
Fax Number: None
Web Site: www.llantwit-football.com
E-mail: chairlffcman@yahoo.com

GENERAL INFORMATION

Social Club Telephone Nº: (01443) 207393
Car Parking: At the ground
Coach Parking: At the ground
Nearest Railway Station: Trefforest (2½ miles)
Nearest Bus Station: Pontypridd (4 miles)
Nearest Police Station: Church Village

GROUND INFORMATION

Ground Capacity: 1,000
Seating Capacity: None
Record Attendance: Approximately 300 (1972)
Pitch Size: 110 x 80 yards

ADMISSION INFO (2003/2004 PRICES)

Adult Standing: £1.00 (by programme)
Child Standing: Free of charge
Programme Price: Included with admission

DISABLED SUPPORTERS INFORMATION

Wheelchairs: Accommodated
Disabled Toilets: Available in nearby Community Centre
Contact Number: (01443) 671971

Travelling Supporters' Information:
Routes: Exit the M4 at Junction 32 and take the A470 towards Pontypridd. Take the exit at the North end of the Trefforest Industrial Estate, cross the River Taff and proceed up Power Station Hill to the traffic lights. Turn left onto the A473 and the ground is immediately on the left opposite CP Motors.

NEWCASTLE EMLYN AFC

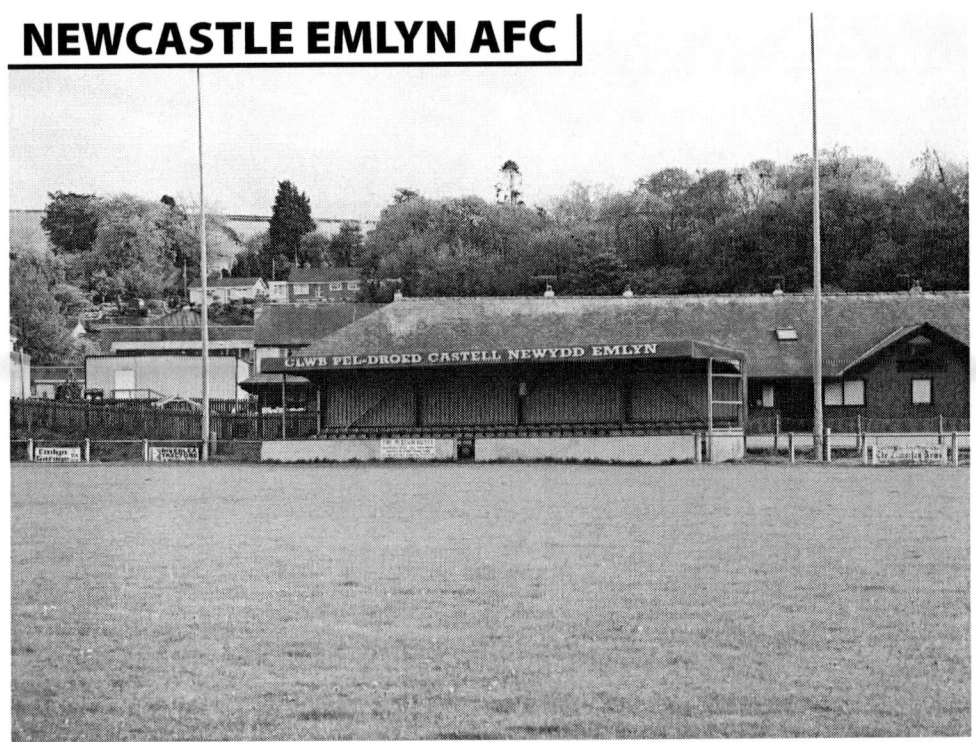

Founded: Before 1912
Former Names: None
Nickname: 'Emlyn'
Ground: Parc Emlyn, Newcastle Emlyn   SA38 9BE
Ground Tel. N°: (01239) 710994
Web Site: www.newcastleemlynfc.com
E-mail: john@newcastleemlynfc.com

Club Colours: Red shirts and shorts
Correspondence: S. John O. Jones, 35 Blaenwern,
Newcastle Emlyn, Carmarthenshire   SA38 9BE
Contact Tel. N°: (01239) 711200
Fax Number: (01239) 710803

GENERAL INFORMATION

Social Club Telephone N°: (01239) 710007
Club Shop: Yes – at the Plough Hotel, Newcastle Emlyn
Car Parking: Adjacent to the ground
Coach Parking: Adjacent to the ground
Nearest Railway Station: Carmarthen (18 miles)
Nearest Bus Station: Newcastle Emlyn (200 yards)
Nearest Police Station: Newcastle Emlyn

GROUND INFORMATION

Ground Capacity: 2,000
Seating Capacity: 120
Record Attendance: 1,800 vs Chelsea (1991)
Pitch Size: 111 x 71 yards

ADMISSION INFO (2003/2004 PRICES)

Adult Standing: £1.50
Adult Seating: £1.50
Child Standing: 50p
Child Seating: 50p
Programme Price: £1.00

DISABLED SUPPORTERS INFORMATION

Wheelchairs: Accommodated
Disabled Toilets: Available nearby
Contact Number: (01239) 710994

Travelling Supporters' Information:
Routes: On reaching Newcastle Emlyn, travel through the outskirts of the town until you reach a junction near a Vauxhall Cawdor Garage. Turn right, travel 100 yards, passing the Plough Hotel by the zebra crossing until you reach the town square near the Central Cafe chip shop. Turn left, then drive straight on and turn into the cattle mart. At the bottom of the large car park, you'll see the ground.

PENTWYN DYNAMOS FC

Founded: 1975
Former Names: Pentwyn & Llanedeyrn Dynamos FC
Nickname: 'Dynamos'
Ground: Cardiff Athletic Stadium, Leckwith, Cardiff
Ground Tel. Nº: (029) 2022-5345

Colours: White shirts with Royal Blue shorts
Correspondence: Malcolm Fraser, 181 Glyn Eiddw, Pentwyn, Cardiff   CF23 7BT
Contact Tel. Nº: (029) 2073-2032
Fax Number: None

GENERAL INFORMATION
Car Parking: 1,600 space car park next to the ground
Coach Parking: Space for 30 coaches next to the ground
Nearest Railway Station: Grangetown
Nearest Bus Station: Cardiff Central
Nearest Police Station: Canton
Police Telephone Nº: (029) 2022-2111

GROUND INFORMATION
Ground Capacity: 5,000
Seating Capacity: 2,500
Record Attendance: Not known
Pitch Size: 110 x 76 yards

ADMISSION INFO (2003/2004 PRICES)
Adult Standing: £2.00
Adult Seating: £2.00
Child Standing: £1.00
Child Seating: £1.00
Programme Price: Included with admission

DISABLED SUPPORTERS INFORMATION
Wheelchairs: Accommodated – Lift access in Grandstand
Disabled Toilets: Available
Contact Number: (029) 2022-5345

Travelling Supporters' Information:
Routes: Exit the M4 at Junction 33 and take the 3rd exit (Leckwith Interchange) signposted for "Athletics Stadium and Leckwith Industrial Estate". Take the 1st exit at the next roundabout onto the B4267 (Leckwith Road). The Stadium us situated on the right after 200 yards.

PONTLOTTYN BLAST FURNACE FC

Founded: 1969
Former Names: None
Nickname: 'The Blast'
Ground: Welfare Ground, Hill Street, Pontlottyn
Ground Tel. N°: (01685) 841305

Colours: Yellow and Green shirts with Green shorts
Correspondence: Barry Horsman, 21 Gelliron, Penpedairheol, Hengoed CF82 8HF
Contact Tel. N°: (01443) 831606
Fax Number: None

GENERAL INFORMATION

Car Parking: Limited number of spaces at the ground
Coach Parking: Available at the local community centre
Nearest Railway Station: Pontlottyn (½ mile)
Nearest Bus Station: Pontlottyn (½ mile)
Nearest Police Station: Rhymney
Police Telephone N°: (01685) 840321

GROUND INFORMATION

Ground Capacity: 1,000
Seating Capacity: None
Record Attendance: 600 vs Newport County (1990)
Pitch Size: 120 x 80 yards

ADMISSION INFO (2003/2004 PRICES)

Adult Standing: £1.00
Child Standing: Free of charge
Programme Price: Included with admission

DISABLED SUPPORTERS INFORMATION

Wheelchairs: Accommodated
Disabled Toilets: None
Contact Number: (01685) 842770

Travelling Supporters' Information:
Routes: Exit the M4 at Junction 32 and take the A470 towards Merthyr. Leave at the Abergavenny turnoff (A465) and continue until you reach Rhymney. Pontlottyn is about 1 mile further along.

PORTH TYWYN SUBURBS FC

Founded: 1921
Former Names: Burry Port Garden Suburbs FC
Nickname: 'Suburbs'
Ground: Parc Tywyn, Woodbrook Terrace, Burry Port, Dyfed
Ground Tel. Nº: (01554) 833471

Colours: Green shirts with Black shorts
Correspondence Address: Colin Jenkins, 25 St. Mary's Rise, Burry Port   SA16 0SH
Contact Tel. Nº: (01554) 832109
Fax Number: (0155) 832109

GENERAL INFORMATION

Social Club Telephone Nº: (01554) 833471
Club Shop: At the Social Club
Car Parking: At the ground
Coach Parking: At the ground
Nearest Railway Station: Burry Port (¼ mile)
Nearest Bus Station: Llanelli
Nearest Police Station: Burry Port

GROUND INFORMATION

Ground Capacity: 1,500
Seating Capacity: None
Record Attendance: 475 vs Llanelli (1998)
Pitch Size: 110 x 75 yards

ADMISSION INFO (2003/2004 PRICES)

Adult Standing: £1.50
Adult Seating: £1.50
Child Standing: £1.00
Child Seating: £1.00
Programme Price: 50p

DISABLED SUPPORTERS INFORMATION

Wheelchairs: Accommodated
Disabled Toilets: None
Contact Number: (01554) 832109

Travelling Supporters' Information:
Routes: From the East: Exit the M4 at Junction 48 and follow signs into Llanelli Town Centre. Pick up the A484 (signposted Carmarthen/Burry Port) and continue along into Burry Port (3 miles). Upon entering Burry Port turn left at the BP Garage (200 yards) and follow the road down the hill. At the bottom of the hill cross over the level crossing and take 1st left then 1st right. The ground is then immediately ahead; From the West: Take the A484 from Carmarthen and in Burry Port turn right at the BP Garage. Then as above.

RISCA & GELLI UNITED AFC

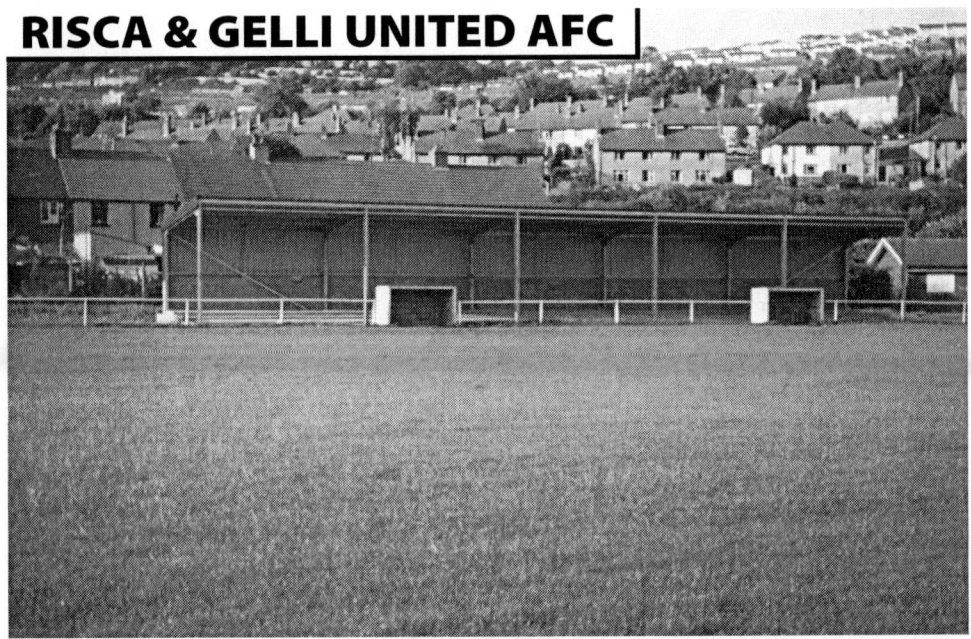

Founded: 1946
Former Names: Risca FC and Gelli FC
Nickname: 'The Cuckoos'
Ground: Ty-Isaf Park, Isaf Road, Pontymister, Risca
Ground Tel. Nº: (01633) 615081

Colours: Black and White striped shirts, Black shorts
Correspondence: Stuart Luckwell, 37 Snowdon Close, Ty-Melin, Risca, Caerphilly NP11 6JF
Contact Tel. Nº: (01633) 615314
Fax Number: (01633) 615314

GENERAL INFORMATION

Club Shop: At the ground – during matches only
Car Parking: Limited number of spaces at the ground – larger car parks available nearby
Coach Parking: One space available at the ground
Nearest Railway Station: Newport
Nearest Bus Station: Newport
Nearest Police Station: Risca (¾ mile)
Police Telephone Nº: (01633) 612391

GROUND INFORMATION

Ground Capacity: 2,000
Seating Capacity: None
Record Attendance: Approximately 2,000
Pitch Size: 110 x 72 yards

ADMISSION INFO (2003/2004 PRICES)

Adult Standing: £2.00
Child Standing: £1.00
Programme Price: Included with admission price

DISABLED SUPPORTERS INFORMATION

Wheelchairs: Accommodated
Disabled Toilets: None
Contact Number: (01633) 615314

Travelling Supporters' Information:
Routes: From the South, East & West: Exit the M4 at Junction 28 and follow the A467 for approximately 5 miles. Leave the A467 at the roundabout signposted for Risca then go straight on at the mini-roundabout into Mill Street. Take the second right for Isaf Road and the ground; From the North: Head for Newport down the Sirhowy or Ebbw Valley from Tredegar, Blackwood and Ebbw Vale. At Crosskeys take the A467 South towards Newport then leave at the roundabout signposted Risca. Then as above.

SEVEN SISTERS AFC

Founded: 1946
Former Names: None
Nickname: None
Ground: Welfare Ground, Church Road, Seven Sisters, Neath, West Glamorgan
Ground Tel. Nº: None

Club Colours: Green shirts and shorts
Correspondence: David Herdman, 79 Main Road, Duffryn Cellwen, Neath   SA10 9LA
Contact Tel. Nº: (01639) 700202
Fax Number: None

GENERAL INFORMATION
Club Shop: None
Car Parking: At the ground
Coach Parking: At the ground
Nearest Railway Station: Neath
Nearest Bus Station: Neath
Nearest Police Station: Neath

GROUND INFORMATION
Ground Capacity: 1,000
Seating Capacity: None
Record Attendance: Approximately 500
Pitch Size: 100 x 65 yards

ADMISSION INFO (2003/2004 PRICES)
Adult Standing: £1.00
Child Standing: Free of charge
Programme Price: £1.00 (includes admission)

DISABLED SUPPORTERS INFORMATION
Wheelchairs: Accommodated
Disabled Toilets: Available
Contact Number: (01639) 700202

Travelling Supporters' Information:
Routes: Exit the M4 at Junction 43 and take the A465 towards Merthyr Tydfil. Turn onto the A4109 Aberdulais and Seven Sisters is about 6 miles along this road. The Welfare Ground is on the right just before you reach the town.

TILLERY FC

Founded: 1910
Former Names: Cwmtillery Excelsiors FC and Cwmtillery AFC
Nickname: None
Ground: Woodland Field, Woodland Terrace, Cwmtillery, Gwent
Clubhouse Tel. N°: (01495) 212310

Club Colours: Red shirts and shorts
Correspondence: Keith Williams, Ashfield House, Ashfield Road, Abertillery NP13 1QE
Contact Tel. N°: (01495) 212497
Fax Number: None

GENERAL INFORMATION
Social Club Telephone N°: (01495) 212310
Club Shop: None
Car Parking: Limited number of spaces at the ground with a larger car park 500 yards away
Coach Parking: 500 yards from the ground
Nearest Railway Station: Abergavenny (14 miles)
Nearest Bus Station: Abertillery (1 mile)
Nearest Police Station: Abertillery
Police Telephone N°: (01495) 212021

GROUND INFORMATION
Ground Capacity: 1,000
Seating Capacity: None
Record Attendance: Approximately 400
Pitch Size: 110 x 65 yards

ADMISSION INFO (2003/2004 PRICES)
Adult Standing: £1.00
Child Standing: 50p
Programme Price: £1.00

DISABLED SUPPORTERS INFORMATION
Wheelchairs: Accommodated
Disabled Toilets: Available
Contact Number: (01495) 212497

Travelling Supporters' Information:
Routes: From the South: Exit the M4 at Junction 28 and take the A467 North to Abertillery. The ground is situated in Cwmtillery, just to the North of Abertillery; From the North: Take the Heads of the Valley Road A465 to Brynmawr then the A467 South to Abertillery for the ground.

TREOWEN STARS FC

Founded: 1926
Former Names: None
Nickname: 'Stars'
Ground: Bush Park, Uplands, Newbridge, Gwent
Ground Telephone Nº: (01495) 248249

Colours: Blue and White striped shirts, Black shorts
Correspondence: B. Huish, 9 Tredomen Terrace, Ystrad Menach, Hengoed CF82 7BW
Contact Telephone Nº: (01443) 813628
Fax Number: None

GENERAL INFORMATION

Club Shop: None
Car Parking: At the ground
Coach Parking: At the ground
Nearest Railway Station: Pontypool
Nearest Bus Station: Newbridge
Nearest Police Station: Newbridge
Police Telephone Nº: –

GROUND INFORMATION

Ground Capacity: 700
Seating Capacity: None
Record Attendance: Not known
Pitch Size: 110 x 72 yards

ADMISSION INFO (2003/2004 PRICES)

Adult Standing: £2.00 (by programme)
Child Standing: £1.00 (by programme)
Concessionary Standing: £1.00 (by programme)
Programme Price: Included with admission

DISABLED SUPPORTERS INFORMATION

Wheelchairs: Accommodated
Disabled Toilets: None
Contact Number: (01495) 248249

Travelling Supporters' Information:
Routes: Take the A467 to Newbridge Town Centre and then follow the road to the Homeleigh Estate. Bush Park is situated in the Uplands area.

TROEDYRHIW FC

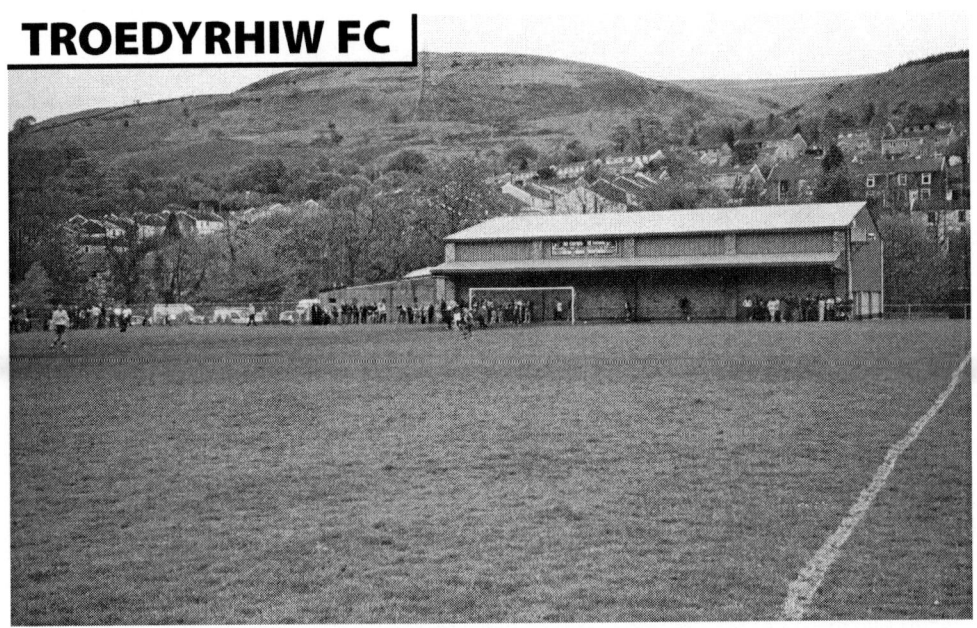

Founded: Early 1900s
Former Names: None
Nickname: 'Rhiw'
Ground: The Willows, Troedyrhiw, Merthyr Tydfil
Clubhouse Tel. Nº: (01443) 692198

Colours: Red and Black striped shirts, Black shorts
Correspondence: Roger Howells, 16 South View, Troedyrhiw, Merthyr Tydfil CF48 4JA
Contact Tel. Nº: (01443) 693857
Fax Number: None

GENERAL INFORMATION
Social Club Telephone Nº: (01443) 692198
Club Shop: None
Car Parking: 50 spaces available at the ground
Coach Parking: At the ground
Nearest Railway Station: Troedyrhiw (200 yards)
Nearest Bus Station: Troedyrhiw (75 yards)
Nearest Police Station: Troedyrhiw
Police Telephone Nº: (01443) 690805

GROUND INFORMATION
Ground Capacity: 1,000
Seating Capacity: None
Record Attendance: Approximately 425
Pitch Size: 100 x 64 yards

ADMISSION INFO (2003/2004 PRICES)
Adult Standing: £1.50
Senior Citizen Standing: £1.00
Child Standing: 50p
Programme Price: Included with admission price

DISABLED SUPPORTERS INFORMATION
Wheelchairs: Accommodated
Disabled Toilets: Available at the Willows Community Centre next to the changing rooms
Contact Number: (01443) 691961

Travelling Supporters' Information:
Routes: Take the A470 towards Merthyr Tydfil then the B4054 to Troedyrhiw. The ground is situated between the River Taff and the railway line, opposite the Police Station.

WALES INTERNATIONAL LINE-UPS AND STATISTICS 2002

13th February 2002
v ARGENTINA *Millennium Stadium*

P. Jones	Southampton (sub. M. Crossley)
M. Delaney	Aston Villa
G. Speed	Newcastle United
A. Melville	Fulham
R. Page	Sheffield United
M. Pembridge	Everton (sub. C. Robinson)
R. Savage	Leicester City
C. Bellamy	Newcastle United
J. Hartson	Celtic
S. Davies	Tottenham Hotspur
R. Giggs	Man. United (sub. J. Robinson)

Result 1-1   Bellamy

27th March 2002
v CZECH REPUBLIC *Millennium Stadium*

D. Ward	Nottingham Forest (sub. D. Coyne)
M. Delaney	Aston Villa
D. Gabbidon	Cardiff City
A. Melville	Fulham
R. Page	Sheffield United
J. Robinson	Charlton Athletic
J. Koumas	Tranmere Rovers
R. Savage	Leicester City (sub. P. Evans)
J. Hartson	Celtic (sub. G. Taylor)
N. Blake	Wolves (sub. P. Trollope)
S. Davies	Tottenham Hotspur

Result 0-0

14th May 2002
v GERMANY *Millennium Stadium*

M. Crossley	Middlesbrough
M. Delaney	Aston Villa
G. Speed	Newcastle United
A. Melville	Fulham
R. Page	Sheffield United
M. Pembridge	Everton
R. Earnshaw	Cardiff City (sub. C. Coleman)
R. Savage	Leicester City
J. Hartson	Celtic
S. Davies	Tottenham Hotspur
R. Giggs	Manchester United

Result 1-0   Earnshaw

21st August 2002
v CROATIA *Varazdin*

P. Jones	Southampton
M. Delaney	Aston Villa
D. Barnard	Grimsby Town (sub. R. Weston)
A. Melville	Fulham
D. Gabbidon	Cardiff City
M. Pembridge	Everton
R. Earnshaw	Cardiff City
A. Johnson	West Bromwich Albion
J. Hartson	Celtic (sub. G. Taylor)
S. Davies	Tottenham Hotspur
C. Robinson	Portsmouth (sub. P. Evans)

Result 1-1   Davies

7th September 2002
v FINLAND (ECQ) *Helsinki*

P. Jones	Southampton
M. Delaney	Aston Villa
G. Speed	Newcastle United
A. Melville	Fulham
D. Gabbidon	Cardiff City
M. Pembridge	Everton
R. Savage	Birmingham City
A. Johnson	West Brom. Albion (sub. C. Bellamy)
J. Hartson	Celtic
S. Davies	Tottenham Hotspur
R. Giggs	Manchester United

Result 2-0   Hartson, Davies

16th October 2002
v ITALY (ECQ) *Millennium Stadium*

P. Jones	Southampton
M. Delaney	Aston Villa
A. Melville	Fulham
D. Gabbidon	Cardiff City
G. Speed	Newcastle United
S. Davies	Tottenham Hotspur
R. Savage	Birmingham City
M. Pembridge	Everton
R. Giggs	Manchester United
C. Bellamy	Newcastle United (sub. N. Blake)
J. Hartson	Celtic

Result 2-1   Davies, Bellamy

WALES INTERNATIONAL LINE-UPS AND STATISTICS 2002-2003

20th November 2002
v AZERBAIJAN (ECQ)   *Baku*

P. Jones	Southampton
M. Delaney	Aston Villa (sub. R. Weston)
A. Melville	Fulham
R. Page	Sheffield United
D. Barnard	Grimsby Town
S. Davies	Tottenham Hotspur
G. Speed	Newcastle United
C. Robinson	Portsmouth (sub. P. Trollope)
R. Giggs	Manchester United
J. Hartson	Celtic
R. Earnshaw	Cardiff City (sub. N. Roberts)

Result 2-0   Speed, Hartson

12th February 2003
v BOSNIA-HERZEGOVINA
Millennium Stadium

D. Ward	Nottingham Forest (sub. M. Crossley)
R. Weston	Cardiff City (sub. M. Jones)
A. Melville	Fulham
R. Page	Sheffield United
G. Speed	Newcastle United
C. Bellamy	Newcastle United
S. Davies	Tottenham Hotspur
R. Savage	Birmingham City (sub. J. Oster)
M. Pembridge	Everton
R. Earnshaw	Cardiff City (sub. J. Koumas)
J. Hartson	Celtic (sub. G. Taylor)

Result 2-2   Earnshaw, Hartson

29th March 2003
v AZERBAIJAN (ECQ)   *Millennium Stadium*

P. Jones	Southampton
J. Oster	Sunderland
G. Speed	Newcastle United (sub. J. Trollope)
A. Melville	Fulham
R. Page	Sheffield United
M. Pembridge	Everton
R. Savage	Birmingham City (sub. C. Robinson)
C. Bellamy	Newcastle United (sub. R. Edwards)
J. Hartson	Celtic
S. Davies	Tottenham Hotspur
R. Giggs	Manchester United

Result 4-0   Bellamy, Speed, Hartson, Giggs

26th May 2003
v U.S.A.   *San Jose*

P. Jones	Southampton (sub. D. Ward)
M. Jones	No club
A. Melville	Fulham
A. Williams	Reading
D. Vaughan	Crewe Alexandra
A. Johnson	West Bromwich Albion
S. Davies	Tottenham Hotspur
J. Koumas	West Bromwich Albion
M. Pembridge	Everton (sub. C. Robinson)
J. Oster	Sunderland (sub. D. Pipe)
G. Taylor	Burnley (sub. N. Roberts)

Result 0-2

WALES AMATEUR INTERNATIONAL LINE-UPS & STATISTICS 2003

UNIBOND SEMI-PROFESSIONAL HOME CHAMPIONSHIP 2003

In May 2003, the Four-Nation Semi-Professional Tournament was played in Wales between teams from Wales, England, Scotland and the Republic of Ireland.

However, the hosts who were winners in 2002 failed to reproduce their previous season's exploits and were awarded the Wooden Spoon!

20th May 2002

v SCOTLAND SEMI-PRO *Carmarthen*

T. Pennock	Farnborough Town
L. Jarman	Barry Town
T. James	Hereford United
S. Evans	Total Network Solutions
L. Phillips	Barry Town
R. Evans	Bangor City (sub. K. Evans)
B. Davies	Chester City
P. Parry	Hereford United (sub. M. Dodds)
G. Lloyd	Barry Town
G. Evans	Caersws (sub. G. Shephard)
P. Smith	Telford United

Result 2-1 L. Phillips, G. Evans

22nd May 2003

v ENGLAND SEMI-PRO *Merthyr Tydfil*

T. Pennock	Farnborough Town
L. Phillips	Barry Town
G. Lloyd	Barry Town
T. James	Hereford United (sub. A. Thomas)
S. Evans	Total Network Solutions
L. Jarman	Barry Town
B. Davies	Chester City
P. Smith	Telford United (sub. M. Dodds)
G. Evans	Caersws
R. Evans	Bangor City (sub. K. Evans)
P. Parry	Hereford United

Result 0-2

24th May 2003

v REPUBLIC OF IRELAND SEMI-PRO

Haverfordwest

L. Kendall	Haverfordwest County
A. Thomas	Newport County
L. Jarman	Barry Town
S. Evans	Total Network Solutions
G. Lloyd	Barry Town
B. Davies	Chester City
K. Evans	Merthyr Tydfil (sub. P. Smith)
N. Davies	Newport County (sub. B. Morgan)
M. Dodds	Port Talbot Town (sub. R. Evans)
G. Evans	Caersws
P. Parry	Hereford United

Result 0-2

The following match was also played during 2003:

24th May 2003

SCOTTISH AMATEUR F.A. vs NORTH WALES COAST F.A. XI *Kirkintilloch*

P. Owen	Llandudno
C. Hogg	Caernarfon Town
L. Atherton	Rhyl
G. Horan	Connah's Quay Nomads
T. Edwards	Rhyl
N. Brookman	Rhyl
S. Terry	Connah's Quay Nomads
L. Hunt	Bangor City
C. McGinn	Rhyl
A. Moran	Rhyl
G. Austin	Llangefni Town

Result 2-1 Moran, McGinn

Substitutes:

R. Harvey	Llangefni Town
L. Dixon	Llangefni Town
B. Hughes	Llandudno
G. Caughter	Porthmadog
R. Roberts	Bodedern